New Approaches to God

Jules M. Brady, S.J.

New Approaches to God

Based on Proofs by
Anselm, Aquinas, and Kant

INTRODUCTION by Joseph Bobik

Professor of Philosophy, University of Notre Dame

Genesis Publishing Company, Inc.

North Andover, Massachusetts

Library of Congress Cataloging-in-Publication Data

Brady, Jules M.
    New approaches to God : based on proofs by Anselm, Aquinas, and Kant
/ Jules M. Brady ; introduction by Joseph Bobik.
        p.   cm.
    Includes bibliographical references and index.
    ISBN 1-886670-09-9 (soft : alk. paper)
    1. God--Proof. 2. Anselm, Saint, Archbishop of Canterbury, 1033-1109.
3. Thomas, Aquinas, Saint, 1225?-1274. 4. Kant, Immanuel, 1724-1804.
I Title.
BT102.B65   1996
212'.1--dc20   96-28095
                                                                        CIP

ISBN 1-886670-09-9 softbound

This book was printed in the United States
by Bradford & Bigelow, Danvers, Massachusetts

Published by *Genesis Publishing Company, Inc.*,
1547 Great Pond Road, North Andover, MA 01845-1216
Tel. 508 688 6688; Fax 508 688 8686

ACKNOWLEDGEMENTS:
        *Translation of Psalm 138, published by the Liturgical Press, copyright by The Order of
        St. Benedict, Inc., Collegeville, Minnesota, used with permission of the publisher.*

        *Chapter 4 originally appeared in Ultimate Reality and Meaning: 14 (1991), pp. 132-
        137. Used by permission of the Editor, Tibor Horvath, S.J.*

        *Chapters 7 and 8 originally appeared in the New Scholasticism: 48 (1974), pp. 219-232;
        and 51 (1977), pp. 1-20. Used by permission of the Editor, Dr. Ralph McInerny.*

        *Chapter 10 originally appeared in the Homiletic and Pastoral Review: 40, Nos. 11-12
        (1990), pp. 62-67. Used by permission of the Editor, Kenneth Baker, S.J.*

"Since creatures depend upon God, by observing creatures we can know that God exists."

Thomas Aquinas
De Veritate, ques. 12, art. 3, rep. to obj. 13.

Jules M. Brady, S.J.

Professor of Philosophy

Rockhurst College

Kansas City, MO

Imprimi potest: E. Edward Kinerk, S.J.

Dedicated to my former students

Janet Calhoun

Mary Brady Charles

Karen Collins

Elizabeth Humphrey

Ann Pavlich

Melissa Ruda

CONTENTS

INTRO-
DUCTION

Those who have tried to prove the existence of God have tried to do it in different ways. Some have tried to deduce God's existence from an idea of God. This was a way tried by St. Anselm. God is that than which nothing greater can be conceived. Therefore, it must follow that God exists. Otherwise, God would not be God. Some have tried to prove God's existence from some fact given to sense observation, some fact observed in the world of physical or sensible things. The Five Ways recorded by St. Thomas Aquinas are of this sort. For example, the First Way departs from the observed fact that there are things in the sensible world which are undergoing motions or changes. Therefore, it must follow that God exists, as the cause without which those motions or changes cannot be fully explained. Others have tried to argue for the existence of God from a fact given to introspective experience, a fact in the world of mental things. Such a way is to be found among the ways tried by Descartes. I have in my mind an idea of God as the Supremely Perfect Being. Therefore, it must follow that God exists, as the only possible cause which could have produced that idea in my mind. Such a way, too, is the way which Fr. Brady presents in chapter eight, entitled "A Contemporary Approach to God's Existence." I know by introspective experience that I know a scientific fact. Therefore, it must follow that God exists, as the cause without which my knowing-that-I-know that scientific fact cannot be fully explained.

A more detailed presentation of this argument might serve the reader as a helpful step toward a better appreciation of it in all its details in chapter eight:

• 1. I know by sense observation, with aid from laser beam technology, the scientific fact that the moon is 239,000 miles, on average, from the earth.

• 2. I know by introspection that I know this scientific fact.

• 3. Neither an Astronomer, nor a Plato, a Kant, a Positivist, or a Naturalist, is equipped to identify the ultimate explanation of my introspectively experienced knowing that I know this scientific fact, i.e., in short, of my knowing-that-I-know.

• 4. But a realist is so equipped. And he might proceed as follows.

• 5. Either a) my knowing-that-I-know has no sufficient reason,
            or b) it is fully explained
        1) by what I am, my essence, as a human being
      or 2) by my substantial existence,
      or 3) by the sum total of all the degrees of existence possessed
            by finite beings,
      or 4) by Pure and Infinite Existence, i.e., God.

• 6. The disjunction in step 5, just above, is complete.

• 7. As regards 5 a), being is intelligible, i.e., everything has a sufficient reason.

• 8. As regards 5 b), neither what I am, nor my substantial existence, nor the sum total of degrees of finite existence can fully explain my knowing-that-I-know.

• 9. Therefore, it must follow that God, Pure and Infinite Existence, exists as the cause without which my knowing-that-I-know cannot be fully explained.

An intriguing argument, indeed; subtle, artful, ascetic, compelling.

Among the many things he says in chapter eight to make as clear as he can how his argument proceeds, Fr. Brady points out that it has used what Fr. E. Coreth calls the "turn to the transcendental method," the method "made famous by Kant in his *Critique of Pure Reason*," but with a significant difference. That is, whereas both Kant and the argument in chapter eight turn from the object known to the knowing of that object, Kant turns to examine the way one knows the object; and the argument in chapter eight, by way of difference, turns to affirm the introspectively observed activity of knowing-that-one-knows in order to draw out its ultimate implication, i.e., its dependence on Pure and Infinite Existence as on the cause without which it cannot be fully explained.

Fr. Brady's book is, among other things, a subtle and challenging reflection, an engaging meditation, on a number of attempted proofs, and attempted disproofs of attempted proofs, for the existence of God. As Fr. Brady sees it, St. Thomas Aquinas tried, but failed, to disprove what appears to be the argument which St. Anselm recorded in chapter two of his *Proslogium*, i.e., a version of the sort of argument which Kant later called the ontological argument. Aquinas did disprove an ontological argument, contends Fr. Brady, but not Anselm's version. And having done that, Aquinas offered what he took to be acceptable arguments for the existence of God, i.e., the Five Ways, three at least of which, the First and the Second and the Third, are forms of the cosmological argument.

Kant too, argues Fr. Brady, tried to disprove the ontological argument; and, beyond that, the cosmological argument as well. But, like Aquinas before him, as Fr. Brady sees it, Kant offered a disproof (explicitly directed at "the famous ontological argument of Descartes") which cannot touch Anselm's version. Moreover, continues Fr. Brady, Kant's attempted disproof of the cosmological argument cannot touch the versions recorded by Aquinas in the *Summa Theologiae*, i.e., the First, Second and Third Ways, nor can it touch the version which appears in his *De Ente et Essentia*.

Chapter seven is an elaborate and extended attempt to clarify the ever difficult, ever intriguing, ever mysterious Fourth Way of Aquinas -- the way based on the more and less good, true, noble, and other such transcending absolutes. Fr. Brady contents himself here with a modest achievement, that of having "made the fourth way more understandable without claiming, of course, to solve completely the mystery of being."

The argument in chapter eight, from knowing-that-I-know, is challengingly subtle, appropriately ascetic, clearly and persuasively presented, and very likely capable of convincing the careful realist reader. One would like to see Fr. Brady anticipate disproofs of this proof, and then proceed to disprove them; or at least show that they cannot touch it.

One may disagree in various ways with the argument in chapter eight, but one must not ignore it. Together with the argument in chapter nine, from the transcending dynamism of the human mind, which is akin to it in many ways, it should be studied with sustained attention and persevering care. It deserves an abundance of both, as does Fr. Brady's book as a whole.

Chapter ten is a fitting way to bring this book to a close. It shows in a most appealing way how philosophical knowledge about the fact of God's existence, and about what God is (or, rather about what God is not), can have religious value, i.e., "can foster those activities by which a believer talks to God [in prayer]," can serve to draw the believer closer to God, can strengthen the believer's friendship with God. The skeptical believer needs to be told, again and again, that philosophy about God can have religious value.

Joseph Bobik
University of Notre Dame

PREFACE

To the question, "From my knowledge of sensible things can I infer the existence of a First Cause?," in this book I present a two part answer. The first part provides the primary texts of Anselm, Aquinas, and Kant. The second part contains interpretative essays.

In Part I, the texts from Anselm and Aquinas are my own translations. The Kant text is Norman Kemp Smith's excellent English version. Part II's interpretative essays are arranged in seven chapters. Chapter four explains that neither Aquinas nor Kant falsify Anselm's first ontological argument. Chapter five concludes that Kant's refutation of a cosmological argument does not refute that argument in Aquinas because both thinkers have different philosophies. Chapter six describes how a thing visibly in motion is being moved by an Invisible, Unique, First Mover. Chapter seven employs a triple procedure to clarify Aquinas' Fourth Way argument for God's Existence. Chapter eight demonstrates God's Existence according to a recent Thomist's analysis of human intellection. Chapter nine presents a contemporary Thomist's path to God's Existence from the dynamism of the human intellect. Chapter ten shows how to build a bridge between the God of philosophy and the God of religion. In brief, this book expresses my effort to discover in the Universe the finger prints of God.

Finally, I must express my indebtedness to Reverend

Vincent F. Daues, S.J., for all the help he has given me in writing chapter five and chapter eight of this book; to Mrs. Renee McGautha and Mrs. Jan Thompson, for their patience in typing the final manuscript of this volume. I also want to thank Reverend Walter Nesbit, S.J., for his assistance in writing the prologue and chapter six.

J. M. B., S.J.

PROLOGUE

I n order to understand clearly why Anselm's and Aquinas' arguments, as given in this book, are new approaches, I shall present in this prologue the traditional expressions of Anselm's ontological argument and Aquinas' cosmological argument.

ANSELM'S ONTOLOGICAL ARGUMENT

Some authors present this argument as follows.[1] Basing the proof on chapter two of Anselm's *Proslogion*, these authors begin with Anselm's statement, "God is that than which nothing greater can be conceived." The argument continues, "that than which a greater cannot be conceived exists." The reason for this is that it is greater to exist in the intellect and in reality than to exist in the intellect alone. Therefore God exists. These authors claim that the above conclusion proves that God exists only in the intellect, i.e., as an idea. In chapter four I argue that Anselm's ontological argument, taken from Anselm's texts, can be so formulated that it establishes God's existence in the real order outside the mind.

AQUINAS' COSMOLOGICAL ARGUMENT

According to Aquinas, every living material being has six intelligible, interior components: *esse*, essence, form, matter, accident and substance. Because Aquinas' cosmological argument, as well as other arguments given in this book, employ these intrinsic principles, I shall begin by showing how they are answers to three questions about facts of experience.

ESSE AND ESSENCE

How can one act of existing, *esse*, be in many living material things? The answer comes from examining facts of experience. The President of the United States, the horse that won last year's Kentucky derby, and the tree living by the Holocaust Museum in Jerusalem exist. On the other hand, the President *is* a rational animal, an essence. The horse *is* an irrational animal, an essence. The tree *is* a non-sentient organism, an essence. Hence *esse* explains that these three beings are one; and essence is the reason these same beings are many. Therefore, *esse* is an inner component by which a living material being exists. And essence is an interior principle by which a living material being is what it is. Consequently being is an existing essence.

FORM AND MATTER

How can one specific perfection, rational animal, essence, be in many individuals? Again the facts are clear. Mary, Kevin, and Peter are all rational animals. Yet Mary, Kevin, and Peter differ as rational animals. And so, form, an inner component of essence, explains that Mary, Kevin, and Peter are one. On the other hand, matter, the other inner component of essence, is the reason why Mary, Kevin, and Peter are many. Therefore, substantial form, an inner component of essence, gives the specific perfection. And prime matter, the other inner component of essence, limits the form and allows one specific perfection to be in many individuals.

SUBSTANCE AND ACCIDENT

How can one individual have many changes and yet remain the same kind of being? Facts of experience are all around us. Mary studies literature, history, and philosophy — these are changes in quality. Kevin, the boy, becomes a man — a change in quantity. Peter travels to St. Louis, Omaha and Boston — changes in place. Accordingly, substance is the inner reason why Mary, Kevin, and Peter remain one kind of individual during these various changes. And accidents designate the many changes in Mary, Kevin, and Peter. Therefore, substance, an inner dynamic constituent of a living material being, "stands-under" accidents. Moreover, accident, another inner constituent of a living material being, inheres in substance.

ACT AND POTENCY

It should be noted that these three sets of components can be arranged in order as manifestations of act and potency. Since existence, form, and accident are perfections, they can be named acts. Inasmuch as essence, matter, and substance are capacities for receiving perfections, they are potencies. From this it follows that act is perfection; and potency is the capacity for receiving a perfection. Therefore, a living material being may be described according to three orders. In the order of existence, *esse* is act; and essence is potency. In the order of essence, form is act; and matter is potency. In the order of activity, accident is act; and substance is potency. These components are not like wooden parts of a tinker toy; they are dynamic constituents present in every living material being.

Keeping Aquinas' six metaphysical components in mind, the three steps in his cosmological argument, given in *On Being and Essence*, can be understood more easily. First step: In a finite being, a living material being, *esse* and essence are really distinct components because I can know *what* a phoenix is and not know *whether* it is.

Second step: the *esse* of a finite being is continually from another. The reason is that without "another" the finite being would bring itself into existence – clearly a contradiction.

Third step: the *esse* of a finite being is continually from a First Cause in whom *esse* is essence, The Infinite Being. Lacking a First Cause, the only other explanation for the continued existence of a finite being would be an infinite series of causes — again, a contradiction.

Why is an infinite series of causes contradictory? For Aquinas this series describes causes acting now in continual dependence on a First Cause. For example, Rodin's statue, *The Thinker*, continually depends for support on a pedestal. The series becomes infinite by multiplying secondary causes indefinitely with the result that there is no First Cause. Now a series, requiring a First Cause and simultaneously postulating all secondary causes, is contradictory. It would be like a series with an end an no beginning.

In chapter five, I give Aquinas' cosmological argument with two variations. First, I omit the infinite series. Secondly, I explain how Aquinas' argument counters Kant's rejection of the cosmological argument.

PART I
PRIMARY TEXTS

1

ST. ANSELM

1. SAINT ANSELM (1033-1109)

PROSLOGION

INSPIRING THE MIND TO CONTEMPLATE GOD. *Chapter 1*

...For I do not seek to understand in order that I may believe, but I believe in order that I may understand. For this I believe: unless I believe, I shall not understand. *Isa.* vii. 9.

GOD TRULY EXISTS. *Chapter 2.*

Therefore, Lord, You who give understanding to faith; help me, insofar as You know it is advantageous, to understand, as we believe, both that You exist and that You are that, than which nothing greater can be conceived. Now does such a nature not exist, because "the fool said in his heart: God does not exist"? [*Psalm* XIV, 1]. Nevertheless, when this very fool hears me saying "that than which nothing greater can be conceived," he understands what he hears, and what he understands is in his intellect, although he does not understand that "that than which nothing greater can be conceived" exists.

For a thing to exist in the intellect is other than to understand that a thing exists. When a painter conceives what he will later paint, he has it in his intellect, but he does not understand it to exist, since he has not made it. Now truly, when he has painted it, he both has it in his intellect, and he understands it to exist, because he has made it.

Therefore, also, the fool is convinced that "that than which nothing greater can be conceived" exists in his intellect because when he hears these words, he understands them; and whatever is understood is in his intellect. But surely, "that than which a greater cannot be conceived," cannot exist in the intellect alone. For, if it exists in the intellect alone, it can be conceived to exist in reality, which is greater.

If therefore, *that than which a greater cannot be conceived* exists in the intellect alone: *that than which a greater cannot be conceived* is that than which a greater *can* be conceived, but certainly, this cannot be. Therefore, undoubtedly, *that than which a greater cannot be conceived* exists, both in the intellect and in reality.

GOD CANNOT BE CONCEIVED NOT TO EXIST. *Chapter 3.*

God is *that than which nothing greater can be conceived.* Therefore, certainly, You so truly exist that You cannot be conceived not to exist. For something can be conceived to exist, which cannot be conceived not to exist; which is greater than what can be conceived not to exist. Therefore, if *that than which a greater cannot be conceived* can be conceived not to exist: *that than which a greater cannot be conceived* is NOT *that than which a greater cannot be conceived.* But this is impossible. Therefore, *that than which a greater cannot be conceived* so truly exists that it cannot be conceived not to exist.

And You are such, O Lord Our God. Therefore, You so truly exist, O Lord my God, that You cannot be conceived not to exist. And rightly. If some mind could conceive something better than You, the creature would ascend above the Creator, and would judge the Creator: which is very absurd. And, indeed, whatever exists besides You alone, can be conceived not to exist. Therefore, You exist more truly and in a higher degree than all others: because, whatever is other than You does not exist as You do, and therefore exists in a lesser degree. Therefore, why "did the fool say in his heart: there is no God," since it is so evident to a rational mind that You exist in a higher degree than all others? Why, because he is dense and a fool?

HOW DID THE FOOL SAY IN HIS HEART, WHAT CANNOT BE CONCEIVED? *Chapter 4*

How indeed did he say in his heart what could not be conceived; or how could he not conceive what he said in his heart, since it is the same to say in the heart and to conceive?

But, if he truly both conceived, because he said in his heart, and he did not say in his heart, because he could not conceive, there is more than one way in which something is said in the heart or conceived. Therefore a thing can be conceived in two ways. For in one way, a thing is conceived, when *the word signifying it* is conceived; and in another way, when *the thing itself* is understood.

Therefore, in the former way, God can be conceived not to exist; in the latter way, God cannot be conceived *not* to exist. For example, according to the words, fire can be conceived to be water; but according to their realities, fire cannot be conceived to be water. Indeed, no one understanding that which God is, can conceive that God does not exist, even though he says these words in his heart, either with no meaning, or with some erroneous meaning. For, God is *that than which a greater cannot be conceived*. And whoever well understands this, understands that God so exists that the Lord cannot be conceived not to exist. Therefore, whoever understands that God so exists, cannot conceive the Creator *not* to exist.

I thank You, gracious Lord, I thank You; because what I formerly believed by Your assistance, I now so understand by Your illumination, that if I was unwilling to believe that

You exist, I could not *not* understand that You exist.

How and why is God seen and not seen by those seeking Him. *Chapter 14*

... My soul strives to see more, and it sees nothing beyond what it saw except darkness.

That God is greater than can be conceived. *Chapter 15*

O God, You are within me and around me, and yet I do not see You. *Chapter 16*

GAUNILO'S first objection

We may notice what was mentioned above, that that which is greater than all which can be conceived, is said to be nothing else than God. When I hear the word *God*, I can as little conceive it or have it in my intellect according to any reality specifically or generically known to me as I can conceive God Himself. Consequently I can conceive that God does not exist. For neither do I know the reality itself of God nor can I infer it from something similar to it. For you assert that it is such, that nothing else can be like it.

For let us suppose that I hear something said about a human person completely unknown to me, whom I would not know even to exist. Through that special or general knowledge by which I know what a human person is, or what human persons are, I could conceive that human person according to the reality which a human person is. And it could happen, if the individual describing that person to me lied, I would conceive of a human person who did not exist; nevertheless I would conceive such a human person as real who would not be that person but any person.

Therefore, I cannot, in the way in which I have the not existing person in my conceiving or in my intellect, have God in my conceiving or in my intellect when I hear the word "God" or the words "something greater than all." For I can conceive of the human person according to a reality known to me, but I can conceive of "God" or "something greater than all," only according to the word. But I can never conceive anything according to the word alone.

ST. ANSELM'S FIRST REPLY

Your careful proof that *that than which a greater cannot be conceived* is not like the unpainted picture in the intellect of the painter, is not my view. For I presented the preconceived painting not to assert that *that than which a greater cannot be conceived* is like it, but only to show that something may exist in the intellect which might not be understood to exist in reality.

Again you say that having heard "that than which a greater cannot be conceived," you can neither conceive it according to any reality known to you generically or specifically nor have it in your intellect, since you neither know such a reality nor can you infer it from a similar reality.

Obviously this is not true. For since every less good, in so far as it is good, is similar to a greater good, it is clear to any rational mind that, by ascending from lesser goods to greater goods, we can conceive something greater and we can infer *that than which nothing greater can be conceived*.

For example, who cannot conceive this, even if he does not believe that what he conceives exists in reality, namely, if there is some good which has a beginning and an end, that good is much better, which has a beginning and no end? And as the latter is better than the former, so that good is better which has no beginning, no end, even if it always passes from the past through the present to the future. And whether some good of this kind is in reality or not, even better still is that good which in no way needs or is forced to change or move.

Cannot this be conceived, or can something greater than this be conceived? Or is not this from those things than which a greater can be conceived to infer *that than which a greater cannot be conceived*? There is, therefore, a way of inferring *that than which a greater cannot be conceived*.

Thus, easily can the fool who does not accept sacred authority be refuted, if he denies that he can infer from other things "that than which a greater cannot be conceived." But if any Catholic denies this, let him remember that "since the creation of the world through understanding those things that are made, the invisible things of God are perceived clearly, even his eternal power and deity." *Romans i. 20.*

GAUNILO'S SECOND OBJECTION

Therefore, when I hear and understand someone saying, "There is something greater than all things which can be conceived," it is certain that "this something" is in my intellect. For this reason, accordingly, that supreme nature is said to exist already in my intellect.

That this nature necessarily exists in reality is proved to me as follows: if it did not exist in reality, whatever exists in reality will be greater than it. And consequently, whatever certainly had already been proved to exist in the intellect will not be greater than all.

To this I reply: if something which cannot be conceived according to any reality, must be said to exist in the intellect: I do not deny that this something exists in my intellect in this way. But because from its existence in my *intellect* I can in no way conclude to its existence in *reality*, I do not as yet entirely grant it existence in reality, until this is proved to me by a certain argument.

Whoever says it exists because otherwise what is greater than all will not be greater than all, does not attend sufficiently to the topic under discussion. For I do not yet say, but I even doubt or deny that it is greater than any reality. I do not concede to it an existence other than (if it must be called existence) the existence a thing has when the soul, only according to a word heard, tries to imagine a thing completely unknown to it.

ST ANSELM'S SECOND REPLY

Moreover, you think, that because *something than which a greater cannot be conceived* is understood, it does not follow that it exists in the intellect, nor if it is in the intellect does it follow that it exists in reality.

To this, I certainly say: if it even can be conceived to exist, it necessarily exists in reality. For "that than which a greater cannot be conceived" cannot be conceived to exist unless without a beginning. But whatever can be conceived to exist and does not exist, can be conceived to exist with a beginning. Therefore "that than which a greater cannot be conceived" cannot be conceived to exist and not exist. Therefore, if it can be conceived to exist, it necessarily exists.

Further: if "that than which a greater cannot be conceived" can be conceived, it necessarily exists. For all who deny that "that than which a greater cannot be conceived" exists, admit that if it existed, it could not not exist either in reality or in the intellect. For if it can be conceived not to exist, it would not be *that than which a greater could not be conceived*. But whatever can be conceived and does not exist, if there were such, it could not exist either in reality or in the intellect. Therefore if "that than which a greater cannot be conceived" can be conceived, it cannot not exist.

But we may suppose, that "that than which a greater cannot be conceived" does not exist, if it can be conceived. But whatever can be conceived and does not exist, if it existed, would not be "that than which a greater cannot be conceived." If therefore "that, than which a greater cannot be conceived" did not exist, it would not be "that than which a greater cannot be conceived" which is absurd. Therefore it is false that *that than which a greater cannot be conceived* does not exist, even if it can be conceived; therefore, much more, if it can be understood or can be in the intellect.

GAUNILO'S THIRD OBJECTION

For example, they say that somewhere in the ocean there is an island, which, due to the difficulty or rather the impossibility of discovering what does not exist, they call the "lost island." They say this island has more riches and more delights than the Islands of the Blessed; and that having no owner or inhabitant, it surpasses completely, in abundance of riches, all the other lands which human persons inhabit.

If someone should tell me such an island exists, I should easily and without difficulty understand the conversation. But suppose then this same person continued to say, "You cannot doubt that this island, more excellent than all other lands, truly exists somewhere in reality, since you do not doubt that it exists in your intellect. And because it is more excellent to exist not in the intellect alone but also in reality; therefore the island necessarily exists. For if it does not exist, any land existing in reality will be more excellent than it. Consequently, the very island, already understood by you to be more excellent than all other lands, will not be more excellent."

If someone by this argument would try to convince me that without any doubt this island exists, either I would think such a person is joking, or I do not know whom I ought to think the greater fool: *I*, if I accepted this proof, or *the other person*, if that person thought that the argument had established the existence of this island with any certitude. To achieve this certitude, the proof would have first to show that the excellence of this island is a truly and indubitably existing thing, and in no way something false and uncertain in my intellect.

ST. ANSELM'S THIRD REPLY

First, you often repeat that I claim that because *what is greater than all* is in the intellect, it must also exist in reality, for otherwise *what is greater than all* would not be greater than all.

Nowhere in my entire writings is there such a demonstration. For *what is greater than all* cannot be proved to exist in reality in the same way as *that than which a greater cannot be conceived* can be proved to exist in reality.

If someone should say that that, than which a greater cannot be conceived does not exist in reality, or can not exist, or can be conceived not to exist, such a person easily can be refuted. For what does not exist, can not exist; and what can not exist, can be conceived not to exist. But whatever can be conceived not to exist, if it exists, is not that, than which a greater cannot be conceived. But if it does not exist, even if it existed, it would not be that, than which a greater cannot be conceived. But it cannot be said that that, than which a greater cannot be conceived, if it exists, is not that, than which a greater cannot be conceived; or if it existed, it would not be that, than which a greater cannot be conceived.

It is evident therefore that neither does it not exist, nor can it not exist, nor can it be conceived not to exist. For if it does not exist, it is not that, than which a greater cannot be conceived; and if it did not exist, it would not be that, than which a greater cannot be conceived.

But, it seems, this cannot be proved so easily of that which is said to be greater than all. For it is not so evident that what can be conceived not to exist is not greater than all which exist, as it is evident that what can be conceived not to exist is not that, than which a greater cannot be conceived. It is deniable that if there is something greater than all, it is that, than which a greater cannot be conceived or that if something greater than all was that, than which a greater cannot be conceived, some other in like manner might be that, than which a greater cannot be conceived. But it is certain that that, than which a greater cannot be conceived is that, than which a greater cannot be conceived.

GAUNILO'S FOURTH OBJECTION

When did I say that *something greater than all* truly exists in reality, in order that from this I could prove that it so exists in reality that it cannot be conceived *not* to exist? For this reason I must first show by a most certain argument that there exists some superior nature, which is greater and better than all which exist, in order that from this we then can infer all those attributes which *that which is greater and better than all* must possess.

When it is said that this highest thing cannot be conceived *not* to exist, might it perhaps be said better that it cannot be understood not to exist or to be able not to exist? For, according to the meaning of the word, false things cannot be understood, which can be conceived in the manner in which the fool conceived God not to exist. And I certainly know I exist, but, nevertheless, I know that I can not exist. But I understand without any doubt that God, who exists in the highest degree, both exists and cannot *not* exist. Whether, however, as long as I most certainly know I exist, I can conceive I do not exist, I do not know. But if I can conceive I do not exist, why do I not know with the same certitude the non-existence of anything else. If I cannot conceive I do not exist, what cannot be conceived not to exist will not be proper to God Alone.

ST. ANSELM'S FOURTH REPLY

But, certainly, this objection to conception is not valid, if one considers the topic well. For, although whatever exists cannot be understood not to exist, all things, except that which exists in the highest degree, can be conceived not to exist. All those things alone can be conceived not to exist, which have a beginning or end or a union of parts, and as I already said, whatever at any place or at any time does not exist as a whole.

That alone cannot be conceived not to exist, in which any conception finds neither beginning nor end nor union of parts, and which conception finds always and everywhere a whole.

Know, therefore, that you can conceive yourself not to exist, as long as you most certainly know you exist. I am surprised that you said you do not know this. For we conceive many things not to exist which we know exist, and we conceive many things to exist which we know do not exist; not by judging them to exist as we conceive them, but by imagining them not to exist or to exist as we conceive them.

And indeed, we can conceive something not to exist, as long as we know it exists, because at the same time we can conceive the former and know the latter. And we cannot conceive something not to exist, as long as we know it exists, because we cannot conceive at the same time that it exists and that it does not exist.

If, therefore, someone distinguishes the meaning of these two sentences, he will understand that nothing, as long as it is known to exist, can be conceived not to exist, and whatever exists, except *that than which a greater cannot be conceived*, even when it is known to exist, can be conceived not to exist.

Thus, therefore, God alone cannot be conceived not to exist; and yet many things, as long as they exist, cannot be conceived not to exist. How, moreover, God can be conceived not to exist, has been sufficiently explained in this little book.

ST. THOMAS AQUINAS

2. ST. THOMAS AQUINAS (1224-1274)

CONCERNING BEING AND ESSENCE

**MANNER IN WHICH ESSENCE IS IN SEPARATED SUBSTANCES.
(DEMONSTRATION OF GOD'S EXISTENCE)** *Chapter 5.*

... Whatever is not included in the understanding of an essence comes to it from without and forms a composite with the essence, because essential components are included in the understanding of an essence. Every essence, however, can be understood without understanding anything about its *esse*. For I can understand what a human person or a phoenix is, and yet not know whether it has an *esse* in the nature of things. Therefore, it is evident that *esse* is other than essence, unless there is something whose essence is its *esse*.

... Whatever belongs to something is either caused by the principles of its essence, as the ability to laugh in a human person, or comes to it from some extrinsic principle, like light in the air from the influence of the sun. The *esse* cannot be caused by the form or essence of a thing as by an efficient cause, because, in this case, something would cause itself and would bring itself into *esse*, which is impossible.

Therefore, every being, whose *esse* is other than its essence, necessarily has its *esse* from another.

... And because everything which is through another, is brought back to that which is through itself, as to the first cause, something must be which is the cause of *esse* in all things, because it is *esse* only. Otherwise there would be an infinite series of causes, since everything which is not *esse* only has a cause of its *esse*.

... And this is the first cause, which is God.

SUMMA THEOLOGIAE

IS GOD'S EXISTENCE ANALYTIC? *Pt. 1, ques. 2, art. 1, c,*

A proposition analytic in itself may be either analytic to us or not analytic to us. For a proposition is analytic when the predicate does not add to the subject, as man is an animal, and animal does not add to man. If the proposition is analytic to everybody, everybody will know the predicate does not add to the subject: as is evident in the first principles of demonstration, whose terms are known to everybody as being and non-being, whole and part. If the proposition is not analytic to some people, the proposition, analytic in itself, will not be analytic to those people. And so, Boethius said that certain propositions are analytic only to the educated, as incorporeal beings are not in place.

I hold that the proposition, "God is," is analytic in itself because the predicate does not add to the subject. For as we shall see, God is His own *esse*. Because we do not know the divine essence, the proposition, "God is," is not analytic to us but must be demonstrated through those things known to us, namely, His effects.

DOES GOD EXIST? *Pt. 1, ques. 2, art. 3, c.*

There are five ways of proving that God exists. The first and most obvious way starts with motion. Our senses testify with certainty that in the world some things are being moved. But whatever is being moved is being moved by another. This is so because whatever is being moved is in potency to that to which it is being moved: whereas, something moves in so far as it is in act. For to move is to reduce something from potency to act; and something can be reduced from potency to act only by a being in act: as fire which is hot in act, makes wood, which is hot in potency to be actually hot, and thus moves and changes the wood. Now it is impossible that the same thing should be simultaneously in act and in potency according to the same aspect, but only according to different aspects. For what is hot in act cannot at the same time be hot in potency, but it can simultaneously be cold in potency. Therefore, it is impossible that according to the same aspect something is both mover and being moved, i.e., that it move itself. As a consequence, whatever is being moved must be moved by another. If the mover of what is in motion is itself being moved, this mover must be moved by another; and this last by another. But this process cannot go on to infinity; because then there would be no first mover, and therefore, no other mover; the reason for this is that secondary movers do not move unless they are moved by a first mover; as the stick does not move unless it is moved by the hand. Therefore, it is necessary to come to some first mover, not being moved by another: and this all understand to be God.

DOES GOD EXIST? *Pt. 1, ques. 2, art. 3, c.*

... The fourth way is taken from degrees which are found in things. For in things there is found something more and less good, and true, and noble: and this is so with other perfections of this kind. But more and less are said of different things according as they approach in different ways something which is the highest: as a thing is hotter the more it approaches the hottest. Therefore, there is something which is truest and best, and noblest, and, consequently, the highest being. For those things which are the highest in truth are the highest in being, as Aristotle says in Book II of the *Metaphysics*. Now what is stated as the highest in some genus, is the cause of all in that genus: as fire, which is the highest heat, is the cause of all hot things, as is said in the same book. Therefore, there is something which for all beings is the cause of *esse*, of goodness, and other perfections of this kind: and this we call God.

WHEN WE DEMONSTRATE THAT GOD *IS*, DO WE AT THE SAME TIME KNOW THE *ESSE* OF GOD? *Pt. 1, ques. 3, art. 4, rep. to obj. 2.*

Esse has two meanings. First, it means the act of existing. Second, it means a logical predicate which constitutes a proposition by positing the subject with its implicit or explicit analytic predicates. Considering the first meaning of *esse*, we cannot know the *esse* of God or His essence. Considering the second meaning of *esse*, we know that the proposition, formed by saying, "God is," is true from the effects of God.

3 IMMANUEL KANT

3. IMMANUEL KANT (1724-1804)

THE CRITIQUE OF PURE REASON

THE IMPOSSIBILITY OF AN ONTOLOGICAL PROOF OF THE EXISTENCE OF GOD

In all ages men have spoken of an absolutely necessary being, and in so doing have endeavored, not so much to understand whether and how a thing of this kind allows even of being thought, but rather to prove its existence. There is, of course, no difficulty in giving a verbal definition of the concept, namely, that it is something the non-existence of which is impossible. But this yields no insight into the conditions which make it necessary to regard the non-existence of a thing as absolutely unthinkable. It is precisely these conditions that we desire to know, in order that we may determine whether or not, in resorting to this concept, we are thinking anything at all. The expedient of removing all those conditions which the understanding requires in order to regard something as necessary, simply through the introduction of the word unconditioned, is very far from sufficing to show whether I am still thinking anything in the concept of the unconditionally necessary, or perhaps rather nothing at all.

Nay more, this concept, at first ventured upon blindly, and now become so completely familiar, has been supposed to have its meaning exhibited in a number of examples; and on this account all further inquiry into its intelligibility has seemed to be quite needless. Thus the fact that every geometrical proposition, as, for instance, that a triangle has three angles, is absolutely necessary, has been taken as justifying us in speaking of an object which lies entirely outside the sphere of our understanding as if we understood perfectly what it is that we intend to convey by the concept of that object.

All the alleged examples are, without exception, taken from judgments, not from things and their existence. But the unconditioned necessity of judgments is not the same as an absolute necessity of things. The absolute necessity of the judgment is only a conditional necessity of the thing, or of the predicate in the judgment. The above proposition does not declare that three angles are absolutely necessary, but that, under the condition that there is a triangle (that is, that a triangle is given), three angles will necessarily be found in it. So great, indeed, is the deluding influence exercised by this logical necessity that, by the simple device of forming an *a priori* concept of a thing in such a manner as to include existence within the scope of its meaning, we have supposed ourselves to have justified the conclusion that because existence necessarily belongs to the object of this concept – always under the condition that we posit the thing as given (as existing) – we are also of necessity, in accordance with the law of identity, required to posit the existence of its object, and that this being is therefore itself absolutely necessary – and this, to repeat, for the reason that the existence of this being has already been thought in a concept which is assumed arbitrarily and on condition that we posit its object.

If, in an identical proposition, I reject the predicate while retaining the subject, contradiction results; and I therefore say that the former belongs necessarily to the latter.

But if we reject subject and predicate alike, there is no contradiction; for nothing is then left than can be contradicted. To posit a triangle, and yet to reject its three angles, is self-contradictory; but there is no contradiction in rejecting the triangle together with its three angles. The same holds true of the concept of an absolutely necessary being. If its existence is rejected, we reject the thing itself with all its predicates; and no question of contradiction can then arise. There is nothing outside it that would then be contradicted, since the necessity of the thing is not supposed to be derived from anything external; nor is there anything internal that would be contradicted, since in rejecting the thing itself we have at the same time rejected all its internal properties. "God is omnipotent" is a necessary judgment. The omnipotence cannot be rejected if we posit a Deity, that is, infinite being; for the two concepts are identical. But if we say, "There is no God," neither the omnipotence nor any other of its predicates is given; they are one and all rejected together with the subject, and there is therefore not the least contradiction in such a judgment.

We have thus seen that if the predicate of a judgment is rejected together with the subject, no internal contradiction can result, and that this holds no matter what the predicate may be. The only way of evading this conclusion is to argue that there are subjects which cannot be removed, and must always remain. That, however, would only be another way of saying that there are absolutely necessary subjects; and that is the very assumption which I have called in question, and the possibility of which the above argument professes to establish. For I cannot form the least concept of a thing which, should it be rejected with all its predicates, leaves behind a contradiction; and in the absence of contradiction I have, through pure *a priori* concepts alone, no criterion of impossibility.

Notwithstanding all these general considerations, in which every one must concur, we may be challenged with a case which is brought forward as proof that in actual fact the contrary holds, namely, that there is one concept, and indeed only one, in reference to which the not-being or rejection of its object is in itself contradictory, namely the concept of the *ens realissimum*. It is declared that it possesses all reality, and that we are justified in assuming that such a being is possible (the fact that a concept does not contradict itself by no means proves the possibility of its object: but the contrary assertion I am for the moment willing to allow). Now [the argument proceeds] "all reality" includes existence; existence is therefore contained in the concept of a thing that is possible. If, then, this thing is rejected, the internal possibility of the thing is rejected – which is self-contradictory.

My answer is as follows. There is already a contradiction in introducing the concept of existence – no matter under what title it may be disguised – into the concept of a thing which we profess to be thinking solely in reference to its possibility. If that be allowed as legitimate, a seeming victory has been won; but in actual fact nothing at all is said: the assertion is a mere tautology. We must ask: Is the proposition that this or that thing (which, whatever it may be, is allowed as possible) exists, an analytic or a synthetic proposition? If it is analytic the assertion of the existence of the thing adds nothing to the thought of the thing; but in that case either the thought, which is in us, is the thing itself, or we have presupposed an existence as belonging to the realm of the possible, and have then, on that pretext, inferred its existence from its internal possibility – which is nothing but a miserable tautology. The word "reality," which in the concept of the thing sounds other than the word "existence" in the concept of the predicate, is of no avail in meeting this objection. For if all positing (no matter what it may be that is posited) is entitled reality, the thing with all its predicates is already posited in the concept of the subject, and is assumed as actual; and in the predicate this is merely repeated. But if, on the other hand, we admit, as every reasonable person must, that all existential propositions are synthetic, how can we profess to maintain that the predicate of existence cannot be rejected without contradiction? This is a feature which is found only in analytic propositions, and is indeed precisely what constitutes their analytic character.

I should have hoped to put an end to these idle and fruitless disputations in a direct manner, by an accurate determination of the concept of existence, had I not found that the illusion which is caused by the confusion of a logical with a real predicate (that is, with a predicate which determines a thing) is almost beyond correction. Anything we please can be made to serve as a logical predicate; the subject can even be predicated of itself; for logic abstracts from all content. But a determining predicate is a predicate which is added to the concept of the subject and enlarges it. Consequently, it must not be already contained in the concept.

"Being" is obviously not a real predicate; that is, it is not a concept of something which could be added to the concept of a thing. It is merely the positing of a thing, or of certain determinations, as existing in themselves. Logically, it is merely the copula of a judgment. The proposition, "God is omnipotent," contains two concepts, each of which has its object – God and omnipotence. The small word "is" adds no new predicate, but only serves to posit the predicate in its relation to the subject. If, now, we take the subject (God) with all its predicates (among which is omnipotence), and say "God is," or "There is a God," we attach no new predicate to the concept of God, but only posit the subject in itself with all its predicates, and indeed posit it as being an object that stands in relation to my concept. The content of both must be one and the same; nothing can have been added to the concept, which expresses merely what is possible, by my thinking its object (through the expression "it is") as given absolutely.

Otherwise stated, the real contains no more than the merely possible. A hundred real thalers do not contain the least coin more than a hundred possible thalers. For as the latter signify the concept, and the former the object and the positing of the object, should the former contain more than the latter, my concept would not, in that case, express the whole object, and would not therefore be an adequate concept of it. My financial position is, however, affected very

differently by a hundred real thalers than it is by the mere
concept of them (that is, of their possibility). For the object,
as it actually exists, is not analytically contained in my concept, but is added to my concept (which is a determination
of my state) synthetically; and yet the conceived hundred
thalers are not themselves in the least increased through
thus acquiring existence outside my concept.

By whatever and by however many predicates we
may think a thing – even if we completely determine it –
we do not make the least addition to the thing when we
further declare that this thing is. Otherwise, it would not
be exactly the same thing that exists, but something more
than we had thought in the concept; and we could not,
therefore, say that the exact object of my concept exists. If
we think in a thing every feature of reality except one, the
missing reality is not added by my saying that this defec-
tive thing exists. On the contrary, it exists with the same
defect with which I have thought it, since otherwise what
exists would be something different from what I thought.
When, therefore, I think a being as the supreme reality, without any defect, the question still remains whether it exists
or not. For though, in my concept, nothing may be lacking
of the possible real content of a thing in general, something
is still lacking in its relation to my whole state of thought,
namely, that knowledge of this object is also possible *a posteriori*.

And here we find the source of our present difficulty.
Were we dealing with an object of the senses, we could not
confound the existence of the thing with the mere concept
of it. For through the concept the object is thought only as
conforming to the universal conditions of possible empirical knowledge in general, whereas through its existence it
is thought as belonging to the context of experience as a
whole. In being thus connected with the content of experience as a whole, the concept of the object is not, however,
in the least enlarged; all that has happened is that our
thought has thereby obtained an additional possible perception. It is not, therefore, surprising that, if we attempt to
think existence through the pure category alone, we can-

not specify a single mark distinguishing it from mere possibility.

Whatever, therefore, and however much, our concept of an object may contain, we must go outside it, if we are to ascribe existence to the object. In the case of objects of the senses, this takes place through their connection with some one of our perceptions, in accordance with empirical laws. But in dealing with objects of pure thought, we have no means whatsoever of knowing their existence, since it would have to be known in a completely *a priori* manner. Our consciousness of all existence (whether immediately through perception, or mediately through inferences which connect something with perception) belongs exclusively to the unity of experience; any [alleged] existence outside this field, while not indeed such as we can declare to be absolutely impossible, is of the nature of an assumption which we can never be in a position to justify.

The concept of a supreme being is in many respects a very useful idea; but just because it is a mere idea, it is altogether incapable, by itself alone, of enlarging our knowledge in regard to what exists. It is not even competent to enlighten us as to the possibility of any existence beyond that which is known in and through experience. The analytic criterion of possibility, as consisting in the principle that bare positives (realities) give rise to no contradiction, cannot be denied to it. But since the realities are not given to us in their specific characters, since even if they were, we should still not be in a position to pass judgment; since the criterion of the possibility of synthetic knowledge is never to be looked for save in experience, to which the object of an idea cannot belong, the connection of all real properties in a thing is a synthesis, the possibility of which we are unable to determine *a priori*. And thus the celebrated Leibniz is far from having succeeded in what he plumed himself on achieving – the comprehension *a priori* of the possibility of this sublime ideal being.

The attempt to establish the existence of a supreme being by means of the famous ontological argument of Descartes is therefore merely so much labour and effort lost;

we can no more extend our stock of [theoretical] insight by mere ideas, than a merchant can better his position by adding a few noughts to his cash account.

PART II
INTERPRETATIVE ESSAYS

4

AN ONTO-LOGICAL ARGUMENT

AN ONTOLOGICAL ARGUMENT FOR THE EXISTENCE OF GOD: ANSELM, AQUINAS, AND KANT IN DISPUTE

In order to make Anselm's first ontological argument more understandable, I propose to question whether Aquinas and Kant's rejection of ontological arguments actually refutes that argument of Anselm. It is well known that Anselm's first ontological argument for God's existence is presented in the second chapter of the Saint's *Proslogion*. In the second question of *Summa of theology*, without mentioning St. Anselm's name, Aquinas does not accept an ontological argument. In *Critique of Pure Reason* Kant, of course, invalidates an ontological argument. To put my inquiry another way, are the above three ontological arguments univocal or analogous?

To achieve my goal I shall divide this chapter into four parts. First, I shall scrutinize Anselm's first ontological argument. Second, I shall determine whether Aquinas' disposal of an ontological argument applies to Anselm's proof. Third, I shall examine the question, Does Kant's criticism of an ontological argument touch Anselm's demonstration. Fourth, I shall conclude by pointing out how Anselm, Aquinas, and Kant view the proposition, God is, the conclusion of demonstrating God's existence.

ANSELM'S FIRST ONTOLOGICAL ARGUMENT

The center piece in resolving the question of this chapter is that Anselm's first ontological argument can be considered on three levels. The first level is the argument taken in the context of chapter two of the *Proslogion*. The second level states the argument abstracted from that context. The third level takes up the demonstration on the second level together with Anselm's rejection of a famous objection by Gaunilo. It is my contention that the above third level containing Anselm's complete first ontological argument will enable me to answer the question raised in this discourse.

The first level of Anselm's first ontological argument – the entire second chapter of the *Proslogion* – illustrates how Anselm applies his formula for studying about God, "It is necessary to believe in order to understand," to his demonstration of God's existence. The last sentence of the *Proslogion's* first chapter expresses the above formula, a union of faith and reason. And the Saint begins chapter two of the *Proslogion* by basing directly on faith the truth of two propositions: God exists; and God is *that than which nothing greater can be conceived*. On this foundation of faith Anselm then uses his understanding to construct his first ontological argument in three propositions. First, God is *that than which nothing greater can be conceived*. Second, but *that than which a greater cannot be conceived* exists. Anselm uses the following reduction to the absurd in order to establish his second proposition. If *that than which a greater cannot be conceived* exists only in the mind: *that than which a greater cannot be conceived* is that than which a greater *can* be conceived. But this is contradictory. Third, therefore God exists. Thus in chapter two by following his formula, it is necessary to believe in order to understand, Anselm demonstrates God's existence.

Upon learning Anselm's first ontological argument, students always ask: "What is the evidence for maintaining that God is *that than which nothing greater can be conceived*?" The answer, of course, is in the first sentence of the

Proslogion's second chapter. There, as I have said, Anselm writes that he believes that God is *that than which nothing greater can be conceived*. The Protestant theologian Karl Barth claims that this combination of faith and reason constitutes a valid argument for God's existence.[1] In short, as Henri Bouillard has shown, Anselm's first ontological argument based on faith is theology, not pure philosophy.[2]

If I omit all reference to faith and simply repeat the syllogism given in chapter two of the *Proslogion*, I shall have the second level of Anselm's first ontological argument. Accordingly, God is *that than which nothing greater can be conceived*. But *that than which a greater cannot be conceived* exists because if *that than which a greater cannot be conceived* exist only in the mind: *that than which a greater cannot be conceived* is that than which a greater CAN be conceived. But this is impossible. Therefore God exists. In the view of some authors of text books on Natural Theology, the above syllogism is Anselm's ontological argument.[3] Since it presents no foundation for *that than which nothing greater can be conceived*, the above syllogism is an incomplete philosophical argument.

The third level of Anselm's first ontological argument is based on a reply given by the Saint to one of Gaunilo's objections. Gaunilo writes that since he does not know the reality of God, he cannot conceive *that than which nothing greater can be conceived*.[4] In responding to Gaunilo, Anselm does not repeat the first sentence of chapter two of the *Proslogion*, that it is by faith that he knows that God is *that than which nothing greater can be conceived*. That would have been to counter a philosophical objection with a theological answer. Instead, Anselm proposes a method of arriving at the concept of *that than which nothing greater can be conceived* by starting with something that is objective, extramental, and in the real order outside the mind, the degrees of good.[5] By ascending from the lesser good, the Saint writes, to the greater good, I can come to the notion of *that than which nothing greater can be conceived*. According to Anselm there are four degrees of good. There is a good which has a beginning and an end. Then there is a good with a beginning and no end. Further, there is a good which has no beginning, no end, but changes. Finally, there is a good lacking beginning, end, and change. This highest degree corresponds with *that than which nothing greater can be conceived*.

I am now prepared to present the third level of Anselm's first ontological argument. By ascending from the lesser good to the greater good, I can form a notion of *that than which nothing greater can be conceived*. On this objective foundation I can proceed to repeat the syllogism given in the first and second levels of Anselm's first ontological argument: God is *that than which nothing greater can be conceived*. But *that than which a greater cannot be conceived* exists in order to avoid the reduction to the absurd given above. Therefore God exists. Henri Bouillard has written that this third level of Anselm's argument, philosophical in content and logical in form, is a complete philosophical argument.[6]

Moreover, this third level of interpretation also achieves Anselm's purpose in writing the *Proslogion*. He expresses this objective in the foreword of that book. There he asks himself "whether it might not be possible to discover an argument that needed no further proof outside of itself and that therefore would alone be sufficient to prove both the existence of God and also that He is the highest good, needing nothing but needed by all in order to be and to be good."[7]

It is appropriate here to consider that "all inadequate concepts of God when their shortcomings are remedied and their contradictions removed lead to what Anselm expressed by 'that than which nothing greater can be conceived.'"[8]

AQUINAS AND THE ONTOLOGICAL ARGUMENT

I can easily answer the question of whether Aquinas rejects Anselm's first ontological argument by noticing if Aquinas' objection to the ontological argument corresponds to the first, second, or third levels of Anselm's first ontological argument. According to Aquinas: From the proposition,

God is *that than which nothing greater can be conceived*, it does not follow that God exists because that would be an illicit transition from a concept in the mind to a reality outside the mind.[9]

Does this illogical passage from concept to reality occur in the first level of Anselm's first ontological argument? The answer, of course, is no. The reason is that in the initial level of his argument, Anselm bases on faith his notion of *that than which nothing greater can be conceived*. On the other hand, Aquinas makes no reference to faith in his objection.

However, there is an invalid passing from concept to reality in the second level of Anselm's first ontological argument. For according to this second level demonstration, without providing a foundation in the real order for the concept, the argument proceeds from the concept of *that than which nothing greater can be conceived* to the existence of God. Hence Aquinas' objection invalidates the second level of Anselm's first ontological argument. This should not surprise me because, as I noted above, on this level the demonstration is an incomplete philosophical argument.

But the third level of Anselm's first ontological argument escapes Aquinas' criticism. For, as I stated before, the argument starts not with a concept but with the objective, extramental degrees of good as a basis for the concept of *that than which nothing greater can be conceived*, and then reasons to the existence of God. And so, I claim that, at this level, Anselm's first ontological syllogism is a complete philosophical argument exempt from Aquinas's objection.

KANT AND THE ONTOLOGICAL ARGUMENT

In order to determine whether Kant's rejection of an ontological argument invalidates the third level of Anselm's first ontological argument, I must explain Kant's dual meaning of "exists," the heart of Kant's denial of an ontological argument.[10] "Exists" for Kant is either "is as a category", a logical predicate, or "exists as experience", a synthetic a posteriori predicate. "Is as a category," like the other eleven categories in the Kantian system, does not present an object but merely connects a subject with explicit or implicit predicates. In Kant's philosophy, "is as a category" posits the subject with its implicit or explicit predicates. For Kant, "is" in the proposition, "God is," is "is as a category", a logical predicate. Also for him, "real" in the statement, "A hundred real dollars is not a penny more than a hundred possible dollars," signifies "is as a category", a logical predicate. On the other hand, Kant maintains that "exists as experience" adds sensation to that space as in the example "a body is heavy." According to him, "real" in the statement, "My financial condition is affected differently by a hundred real dollars than it is by a hundred possible dollars," signifies "exists as experience".

With Kant's twofold explanation of "exists" before me, I can explain readily how Kant discards his own onto-logical argument composed of the following three propo-sitions. First, the concept of most real being contains all re-ality and is possible. Second, all reality includes existence. Third, therefore concept of most real being is. "Is" in the preceding sentence, according to Kant, does not mean "ex-ists as experience", because the latter always signifies sen-sation; and we have no sensation of most real being, God. Consequently, "is" in the sentence, "Concept of most real being is," signifies "is as a category", a logical predicate. Hence the proposition, "God is," is a logical proposition. It can be denied without a contradiction. It follows that for Kant his own formulation of an ontological argument has proved nothing. If the denial of the proposition, "God is," was a contradiction, the proposition would have been ana-lytic since Kant takes the position that an analytic proposi-tion is one in which the predicate adds nothing to the sub-ject with the result that the denial of such a proposition is a contradiction.

This Kantian criticism of an ontological argument does not affect the validity of the third level of Anselm's first ontological argument. As established above, Kant holds that a denial of the conclusion of an ontological argument, "God is," is not contradictory. But for Anselm a denial of the proposition, "God is" – the conclusion of the third level of his first ontological argument – does involve a contradiction. If God does not exist, Anselm's hypothetical proposition, a component of his first ontological argument – if *that than which a greater cannot be conceived* exists only in the mind: *that than which a greater cannot be conceived* is that than which a greater CAN be conceived – would not be the absurdity that it is. And so the third level of Anselm's first ontological argument is free from the Kantian criticism. I must maintain that in Anselm's view, the proposition, "God is" – the conclusion of his first ontological argument on the third level – is an *analytic proposition in a special sense.* Since Aquinas and Kant fail to strike down Anselm's first ontological argument, the ontological arguments of Anselm, Aquinas, and Kant are not univocal, but, at best, analogous.

ANSELM, AQUINAS, KANT: A COMPARISON

For the purpose of understanding how Anselm, Aquinas, and Kant view the proposition, God is – the conclusion of a demonstration of God's existence – I shall ask, in turn, whether these three philosophers would grant that the above proposition is a proposition analytic in itself, a proposition analytic to us, a logical proposition, or an *analytic proposition in a special sense.*

In order to answer the above questions for Anselm, I must recall that an analytic proposition is one in which the predicate does not add to the subject, with the consequence that a denial of the proposition is contradictory. First, Anselm would say that the conclusion of his first ontological argument, "God exists," is analytic in itself. This means that in God essence and the act of existing are the same. This is true for Anselm because in chapter three of the *Proslogion*, the Saint concludes his second ontological argument with the proposition, "God cannot be conceived not to exist." Second, Anselm would not allow the conclusion of his first ontological argument to be analytic to us as is the case with the proposition, "The whole is greater than the part." While we immediately know that the whole is

greater than the part, in this life we do not know the divine
essence. This is clear because in chapter fourteen of the
Proslogion, Anselm writes as follows: "My soul strives to
see more and it sees nothing beyond what it saw except
darkness." Thus Anselm's first ontological argument has
not made God physically present to the Saint. Third, I have
established already that Anselm would not admit that the
conclusion of his first ontological argument is a logical
proposition. Fourth, I have said previously that for Anselm,
the conclusion mentioned in the preceding sentence is an
analytic proposition in a special sense.

Aquinas explicitly answers my four questions in the
first part of the *Summa of Theology*. First, in the initial article
of the second question, he asserts that the proposition, "God
is," is analytic in itself because, in God, essence and the act
of existing are the same. Second, in the same article, he de-
clares that the proposition, "God is," is not analytic to us.
For in this life, we do not know the divine essence. Third,
according to Aquinas, the proposition, "God is," which is
the conclusion of his demonstration of God's existence, is a
logical proposition that is true from effects.[11] Aquinas's most
characteristic demonstration of God's existence, given in
the book *On Being and Essence*, begins with the real distinc-
tion between the essence and the act of existence in a finite
being. He then reasons that from a limited being's act of
existing, the effect, one can argue to the existence of a cause,
Pure *Esse* or God, who continually sustains the limited act
of existing, like the sun continually gives light to the air.
Fourth, since the proposition, "God is," is logical, it cannot
be *analytic in a special sense.*

After calling any other meaning of "exists" than "is
as a category" or "exists as experience" an unwarranted
assumption, Kant would have no difficulty answering my
four questions. He would not allow the proposition, "God
is," to be analytic in itself. For, as I have observed, with
Kant "is as a category" and "exists as experience" refer to
propositions, not to the Deity. Also he would deny that the
proposition, "God is," is a proposition analytic to us because, as I have mentioned, his position is that the above

proposition is a logical proposition. From this it follows that for Kant the proposition, "God is," could never be *analytic in a special sense.*

CONCLUSION

In this chapter I have proved two points. First, neither Aquinas nor Kant manage to falsify Anselm's first ontological argument on the third level. Second, the proposition, "God is," differs in meaning for Anselm, Aquinas, and Kant. Is it any wonder that Anselm's ontological argument has continued to interest philosophers from the time of Gaunilo down to our own times?

THE COSMO- LOGICAL ARGUMENT

5

THE COSMOLOGICAL ARGUMENT: AQUINAS AND KANT

This essay attempts to investigate the often made claim that Kant has disproved Aquinas' demonstration for God's Existence.[1] Accordingly, I shall present a reformulation of Aquinas' cosmological argument for God's Existence[2] before presenting Kant's rejection of a cosmological argument for God's Existence.[3] I shall conclude by showing that the latter refutation does not touch Aquinas' demonstration.

For the sake of clarity, before proceeding I must point out the difference between the cosmological and the onto- logical arguments for God's Existence. In the former, from the existence of the world I reason to the existence of a First Cause. In the latter, from the notion of God I infer the exist- ence of God.

Aquinas' demonstration

Aquinas' cosmological argument emerges from answering three general questions. The first general question involves two separate questions about every finite material being: What is it? And: Is it? The first thing that I directly perceive by the activity of my senses and by the activity of my intellect is the being of sensible things. With my sight, I see the color, size, shape, motion of a sensible thing such as the President of the United States. With my intellect, I know beneath the sensible manifestations that the non-spatial component, essence, of the Chief Executive answers the question, What is he? And the non-spatial component, *esse*, the act of existing, of the President answers the question, Is he? Thus *essence* is a non-spatial inner component of a finite being by which something is what it is; *esse* is a non-spatial inner component of a finite being by which something is.

What a scientist can do, a philosopher can do. Granted that *esse* and essence are non-spatial components, let me call attention to the fact that the famous biologist Hans Driesch sought to find a non-spatial element, *E*, which he named a psychoid, in the embryo to account for the fact that a rabbit embryo developed into a rabbit and not a squirrel.[4]

In order to explain how essence and *esse* of a finite being are not sensible but intelligible, I must distinguish between those things having the conditions of matter from those things or components not having the conditions of matter. The color, shape, size, motion of the President are sensible and thus are examples of the conditions of matter. To put it another way, these sensible appearances constitute the phenomenon of a thing that exists for itself. But the essence and the *esse* of the President are without conditions of matter and are not sensible but intelligible. In other words, essence and *esse* of a finite being are the intelligible connections – a thing that exists for itself – that make up what the intellect discovers beneath the phenomenon.

Further analysis reveals that the essence of the President and his *esse*, the act of existing, are not two really distinct complete beings but rather two really distinct inner components. For everyone would admit that the Chief Executive, the horse that won last year's Kentucky Derby, and the tree growing by the Holocaust Museum in Jerusalem are similar because they all exist. Yet all would agree that the above three individuals are distinct due to their essences.

The essence of the President is a rational animal; the essence of the horse is an irrational animal; the essence of the tree is a living non sentient organism. Besides in a finite being, the *esse* must be distinct from the essence because if I identify the *esse* with the essence of a tree, everything that exists would be a tree.[5] But this is patently false. Hence the essence and the act of existing (*esse*) are distinct inner components, not only of the President but of every finite being. And now the notion of finite being is an existing essence in which there are really distinct, not sensible but intelligible, principles of a finite being.

The second general question required in order to construct Aquinas' cosmological argument is, What sustains the *esse* of the President? The reply to this question depends on a correct understanding of the principle of causality: a cause is both simultaneous with the effect and prior in nature to the effect.[6]

It is easy to understand that the cause and effect are *simultaneous*. When the teacher moves the chair, the chair is being moved – the effect – as long as the teacher – the cause – moves the chair. Once the teacher ceases moving the chair, the chair immediately stops being moved. Thus cause and effect are simultaneous.

The same example illustrates how the cause is *prior* in nature to the effect. This simply means that the teacher – the cause – moves the chair – the effect. However, the chair being moved – the effect – does not move the teacher – the cause. In brief, the cause brings about the effect but not vice versa. And so, the cause is prior in nature to the effect.

With the explanation of the principle of causality before me, I can now proceed to answer the question, Who sustains the act of existence of the President. One explanation is that his parents sustain his act of existing. This cannot be true because, once the parents have died, the President continues to exist. If the parents sustained the President's existence according to the principle of causality (saying that cause and effect are simultaneous), the President should have ceased to exist at their death. But he continues to exist. The parents cannot be the answer.

Perhaps the answer to the question, Who sustains the President in existence, is the President himself. Once again the principle of causality – now phrased as "cause is prior in nature to the effect" – will help me discard the President as the sustaining cause of this continued existence. If the Chief Executive causes his own continued existence, then the cause – his continued existence – is both prior in nature to the effect – which is his continued existence – and this same cause is *not* prior in nature to the effect, since his existence is itself an effect – which is a contradiction.

The rejection of the President's parents and President himself as the sustaining cause of the Chief Executive's existence brings up the third general question in my analysis: Who ultimately sustains the *esse* of the President? Aquinas answers that the ultimate cause of the Chief Executive's existence is the First Cause, a being that is its own existence, a being that transcends past and present, a being in whom the essence and the act of existing are the same: the simple, unique Pure Act of Existing.

With this explanation, I have a cause that is both simultaneous with the effect and also prior in nature to the effect. Simultaneity needs no further explanation because the President continues existing as long as the cause is causing. That the First Cause is prior in nature to the Chief Executive's continued existence is evident since he depends on the Cause, not vice versa.

Now, how do you prove that the First Cause ultimately accounts for the President's continued existence? Since, as I have argued, a finite being, like the President, cannot be its own efficient cause; if there is no Infinite Being, or First Cause, the finite being simply wold not be.[7] To conclude, the not sensible but intelligible existence of the President and of all finite beings is sustained by the not sensible but intelligible First Cause, Pure *Esse*. Of course, in this metaphysics of being, outside of being there is only non-being. And the notion of being that includes both finite and Infinite Being is a not sensible but intelligible existing essence.

KANT'S REFUTATION

Kant's rejection of the cosmological argument may be structured around his answers to three questions. The first question is this: Why does Kant describe knowing as knowing a phenomenon? The necessary causal proposition, "The sun warms the stone," is an example of this phenomenon.[8] His effort to reconcile two presuppositions provides the answer.

The first presupposition is Newton's view that propositions in physics are synthetic and necessary. His conservation of energy law (saying that every material change is accompanied by an unchanged quantity of matter) is an example of such a proposition. This law is synthetic because the predicate, "unchanged quantity of matter," adds to the subject, "every material change."

Kant adopts as his second presupposition Hume's view of knowledge: what I know is a stream of unconnected sensible perceptions, atomic like units, that refer to nothing. Hume had written "when I enter most intimately in what I call *myself*, I always stumble on some particular perception or other, of heat or cold, light or shade. [...] I never can [...] observe anything but the perception."[9]

To explain the conformity of necessary propositions in physics with a stream of unconnected perceptions, Kant examines the conditions of scientific knowledge. The necessity in propositions cannot be explained by the unconnected perceptions because the perceptions are not connected. Then Kant proposes that a faculty of the mind, the understanding, constructs the necessity expressed by the twelve categories of the understanding. Kant then concludes that the object of scientific knowledge must have two components. The first component is matter, which comes from sensation of the thing in itself. It provides the content for knowledge. The second component is form, which arises from the understanding. This form, or *a priori* category, furnishes the necessary connection in the object of knowledge. Thus, knowing the object of scientific knowledge, the phenomenon, signifies knowing matter and form.

By using Kant's synthetic necessary causal proposition, "The orange round sun warms the white square stone", I can detail how the faculties, understanding and sensibility, partially construct the phenomenon. The thing as object, that is, the noumenon, causes sensation – like color, sound, odor, flavor, resistance – to be received by the faculty of sensibility. Hence, the noumenon causes the orange color of the sun and the white color of the stone to affect sensibility. Sensibility then imposes the *a priori* sense form of space on sensation, since space is not given in color, sound, odor, flavor, resistance. And so, sensibility imposes both "round" on the orange sun and "square" on the white square stone. The fact that the latter appearance follows from the first appearance Kant explains by the *a priori* form of time arising from sensibility. Kant then introduces the *a priori* category of causality coming from the faculty of understanding to provide the necessary connection between the two appearances. Hence "warms," necessarily connecting the sun and the stone, is the category of causality.

To sum up, I can reflect on the origin of the four components of the phenomenon: sensation, space, time, category. The noumenon causes sensation to be received by sensibility. Sensibility imposes forms of space and time on sensations to constitute appearances – the matter. The understanding not only connects the two appearances necessarily by a category – the form – but also knows the resulting phenomenon. Therefore, the phenomenon is partially *constructed*, since of the four components of the phenomenon, only sensations are given, while space, time, and category are provided by the faculties. Consequently, in a phenomenon like the causal proposition, "The sun warms the stone," a sensible cause is necessarily connected with a sensible effect.

From Kant's answer to the first question about his description of knowing, I can explain readily how Kant replies to the second question, Why is the cosmological proof for God's Existence in error? Kant views the cosmological proof as arguing that "I exist, therefore an absolutely necessary being also exists."[10] This is based on the principle that "if anything exists, an absolutely necessary being also exists.[10]" But here I infer from a sensible effect, my existence – space and sensation – a not sensible cause – the existence of an absolutely necessary being. However, for Kant the only legitimate expression of the causal proposition is that a sensible effect necessarily follows from a sensible cause. Therefore Kant rejects vaulting from a sensible effect, my existence, to a not sensible cause, an absolutely necessary being.

Kant's claim that his *cosmological* argument leads into the *ontological* argument brings up the third question in my study: how does Kant falsify the ontological argument? In his cosmological argument, Kant maintains that the most I can infer from my existence is a regulative idea of God. But to argue that the idea of God, the idea of a Most Real Being, entails existence is the ontological argument.[11]

In every ontological argument for God's Existence, the denial of the proposition, "God exists," is contradictory. But this is not the case with Kant because he maintains that his two meanings of existence can be denied of God without a contradiction. His first meaning of exists is "is as a category". Here "is" merely posits the subject with all its explicit or implicit predicates as in the proposition, "Triangle is a three angled figure." If I deny that a triangle is, there is no contradiction. Hence if I deny God is – as a category – no contradiction results.[12]

His second meaning of existence is "exists as experience". In this context, "exists" merely adds a sensation to the subject as in the proposition, "A body is heavy." Notice that body is the form of space; and heavy is a sensation. If I deny "God exists as experience", there is no contradiction because "exists as experience" entails space and sensation. But I have no sensation of God. Thus, "exists" for Kant either means "is as a category", one component of the phenomenon, or it signifies "exists as experience", two components – space and sensation – of the phenomenon. Kant adds that "any alleged existence outside this field [...] is [...] an assumption which we can never be in a position to justify."[13]

CONCLUSION

Hence Kant's philosophy is a phenomenology having room only for knowing a phenomenon, a sensible effect necessarily connected with a sensible cause. Not only are phenomenon and noumenon separate, but also the faculties of the mind – reason and understanding – can't know the noumenon. Moreover, "exists" is either "is as a category," one component of the phenomenon, or "exists as experience," space and sensation, two components of the phenomenon.

On the other hand, Aquinas' philosophy is an ontology providing scope for knowing beneath the sensibles – what Kant calls phenomena – the intelligible connection between a not sensible effect, limited *esse*, and the truth of the proposition. Beneath the sensibles, there is a not sensible First Cause, namely Pure *Esse*. Thus Kant's phenomenon/noumenon come to mean in Aquinas' thought, "sensible appearance of the thing that exists for itself."[14] In Aquinas' philosophy, being is either the *finite* noumenon – composed of the act of existing and essence, really distinct not sensible principles of being – or the *infinite* noumenon in which the act the existing and essence are the same, the not sensible Pure *Esse*, the First Cause.

In summary, Kant and Aquinas simply offer us different philosophies; consequently one does not negate the other. Therefore, although some authors may claim that Kant refutes his own view of a cosmological argument, he does not invalidate Aquinas' cosmological argument.

6 | THE FIRST WAY

THE FIRST WAY: AQUINAS AND SMITH

I n order to clarify St. Thomas' "First Way," I propose to answer this following question: How can I really know that a thing which is visibly in motion is in fact moved by an Invisible Unique First Mover, that is, Pure *Esse*? I shall propose a two stage response. First stage: Aquinas argues that a thing visibly in motion is moved by an Invisible but Intelligible First Mover. Second stage: Smith has established that a thing visibly in motion is moved by an Invisible but Intelligible Unique First Mover, that is, Pure *Esse*.

FIRST STAGE: AQUINAS

In his *Summa of Theology*, Part I, question 2, article 3, Thomas proceeds in four steps. First step: It is evident to our senses that in the world a thing is being moved. For example, a tan chair is being moved by me.

Second step: the chair that is being moved is composed of two invisible but intelligible components: potency and act. For the sake of clarity, a brief history of the act/potency theory is in order.

Parmenides noticed that early Greek philosophers,

materialists, said water (Thales), air (Anaximines), and fire (Heraclitus) are the stuff out of which all things are made. Since water, fire, air *are*, Parmenides concluded that One Material Being is the stuff out of which all things are made. Further, Parmenides observed that our *senses* see the appearances of local motion, but our *intellect*, having penetrated beneath these appearances, arrives at Invisible but Intelligible Being. Since visible newness, which appears to result from local motion, can not be explained either by saying that Invisible but Intelligible Being changes to Invisible but Intelligible Being or by asserting that non-being changes to Invisible but Intelligible Being, he concluded that local motion is not possible but an illusion. It is, instead, an illusion for the intellect.

To answer Parmenides, Aristotle taught that local motion is visible but also intelligible because the intellect can know beneath visible local motion the invisible but intelligible components of potency, the permanent element in motion and act, the novelty resulting in motion. Thus, local motion is a transition from potency to act.

Aquinas, following Aristotle, maintains that although I see the color of the chair and the motion from one place to another, my intellect grasps more than my senses do. While my senses put me in touch both with the color of the object and with the fact of movement, my intellect knows that other realities are involved. One of these is called "potency," which may be actuated in various ways. It is the permanent element in motion. The other is "act." This is the element that accounts for change. Accordingly, before motion begins, the chair about to be moved is composed of potency and act_1. While the chair is being moved, the actual motion involves potency and act_2. At the end of the motion, the chair has two constituents, potency and act_3. And so, motion is the transition (potency and act_2) from potency (potency and act_1) to act (potency and act_3). *Potency* is the capacity for receiving a perfection while *act* is the perfection received.

Third step: the tan chair — in motion due to the two invisible but intelligible components, potency and act_2 —

is being moved by a cause containing invisible but intelligible act. Aquinas' argument for this is straight forward. Without a distinct mover that contains invisible but intelligible act, the only other explanation for the continuing act would be that the same being is both being moved or in act_2 with potency for act_3 and, at the same time, the same being is the mover or in act. This is contradictory. Water does not heat itself to the boiling point. Is it not immediately evident that affirmation and denial cannot be true in the same respect simultaneously?[1] Therefore, whatever is being moved (or in potency and act_2) is being moved by a mover containing an invisible but intelligible act.

Fourth step: there is an Invisible but Intelligible First Mover, Pure Act, to avoid an indefinite multiplicity of secondary movers, each composed of potency and act. For secondary movers do not move unless they are moved by a First Mover. This follows from a hypothetical proposition: If there is no First Mover, since I do not totally move myself – my will changes from potency to act – I would not move. Now the consequent of this proposition is false. Therefore the antecedent is false. Aquinas concludes that there is an Invisible but Intelligible First Mover Pure Act.

SECOND STAGE: SMITH

In his *Natural Theology*, Smith presents the second stage of the answer to the initial question by replying to an objection. He objects that Aquinas' First Way establishes not a Unique First Mover but many First Movers.[2] Smith argues as follows. Cold water being heated is being moved ultimately by a First Heater. Harry gaining knowledge is being moved finally by a First Intellect. Ralph running is being moved at last by a First Runner. These three First Movers are in three different categories. Hence Aquinas' First Way concludes with many First Movers.

To answer his objection, Smith proposes that the second step in Aquinas' argument should be augmented to read: The tan chair being moved is composed of three invisible components, that is, existing, potency, and act_2. As a result, the fourth step in Aquinas' proof should conclude with an Invisible First Mover who is Pure Act of Existing, Pure *Esse*. This First Mover is outside the categories. I can easily show that Pure Act of Existing is unique: For two pure acts of existing differ by nothing.

Thus, with the assistance of Aquinas and Smith, I can respond to the question, How can I know that a thing visibly in motion is moved by an Invisible but Intelligible Unique First Mover that is Pure *Esse*? It is with my intellect that I can know beneath the color and motion of the moving object, invisible but intelligible existing, potency and act_2. From this invisible but intelligible existential starting point I can reason to an Invisible but Intelligible Unique First Mover that is Pure *Esse*.

WHY MANY FIRST MOVERS?

Noticing that Aquinas' First Way, complemented with Smith's addition to the text, concludes with a Unique First Mover prompts one to wonder why Aquinas did not write the First Way so that by itself it would establish a Unique First Mover. Edward Sillem, in his *Ways of Thinking about God*, provides an answer that corresponds with the texts of Aquinas.[3]

According to Sillem, Aquinas' purpose in writing the First Way, using only the act potency philosophy of Aristotle and omitting his own philosophy of *esse*, was to teach some Augustinian theologians of his day. These theologians held that we have some kind of direct, immediate knowledge of God's Existence. To counter this assertion, Aquinas, through his First Way text using only Aristotelian philosophy, proposed that even without the benefit of Christian Revelation, Aristotle taught that through knowing sensible motion, we have indirect, mediate knowledge of a First Mover. Aquinas thought that Aristotle's theory was correct as far as it goes, but incomplete.

To corroborate his view that the text of the First Way presents only Aristotle's view, Sillem points out that the entire text of the *Summa of Theology*, Part I, question 2, article 3, containing the famous Five Ways, never explicitly mentions *esse*, with the exception of one use of the term in the Fourth Way text. He further remarks that Philosophy of Religion books, offering only the Five Ways text as Aquinas' arguments for God's existence, do not adequately present Aquinas' view. Is it any wonder that so many philosophers have discredited the Thomistic proofs for God's Existence?[4]

In order to give a complete First Way argument concluding with a Unique First Mover, Aquinas supplements Aristotle's argument with the philosophy of existence. The Angelic Doctor does this in the *Summa of Theology*, Part I, question 3, article 4, where he teaches that in a creature *esse* and essence are really distinct components, whereas in God *esse* and essence are identical, a Unique First Cause.

Thus Aquinas explained to the Augustinians that, by sensory and intellectual knowledge of existing sensible motion, we can have indirect, mediate knowledge that there is a First Mover, who is Pure *Esse*, the Unique God of the Christians.

To summarize, in order to have Aquinas' complete First Way argument, the first paragraph of question 2, article 3 must include the philosophy of existence as contained in question 3, article 4.

THE
FOURTH
WAY

NOTE ON THE FOURTH WAY

his chapter attempts to clarify the reasoning process in Thomas Aquinas' Fourth Way by using a triple procedure: raising a question about different degrees of existing, comparing a grade of existing with quantity, and examining an objection. Certainly, any effort toward making the fourth proof of the existence of God more intelligible, or less unintelligible, seems worthy of merit.

Accordingly, the first aim of this meditation will be to explain the ultimate similarity between a human *esse* and a brute *esse*, different degrees of being. They are proximately similar because both the human *esse* and the brute *esse* are perfections of existing. Yet they differ, since a human entitative act is superior to an animal's ontological act. For whoever admits that as a being exists so does it act, and whoever accepts that human intellection is a strictly immaterial activity – while sensation, the highest operation of a brute, is in some way material – will grant the truth of the proposition not that man is a better man than an animal, not that man is a better animal than a brute, but simply that man has an ontological act which is better than the ontological perfection of an irrational animal.[1] The question raised in this discussion, then, is how do I ultimately explain that a human existential act and a brute existential act, which are dissimilar degrees of existing, are alike. Surely, this is a tantalizing puzzle.

Due to its abstruse character, the point at issue here must be made more precise. In Aristotle's philosophy of nature, two men are similar as men for the reason that each essence has an intrinsic actual principle, substantial form.[2] And it is consistent with Aquinas' philosophy of being to maintain that a man and a brute are similar as being inasmuch as there is a transcendental relation between essence and existence in each of these beings. The question of this study, then, is not how to ground the similarity between two human beings as men, not what is the basis for the resemblance between a man and a brute as being, but what are the credentials for acknowledging the likeness between the act of existing of a man and the act of existing of a brute – which are different degrees of being.

How can a human existential perfection and a brute existential act be both *one,* insofar as they resemble each other, and *many,* insofar as they are diverse? Indeed this is a profound metaphysical consideration.

Further light on the topic under scrutiny can be gained by comparing a real relation of quantity with a real relation of similarity in existing. To affirm that a yardstick is bigger than a one-foot-ruler is to ascribe to them a real relation of quantity. Now any real relation minimally requires three things: a real subject, that which is ordered to the term; a real term, that to which the subject is ordered; and a real foundation, the reason why the subject is ordered to the term. It is obvious, in this quantitative proportion, that the subject, the term, and the foundation are the yardstick, the ruler, and their dimensions respectively.[3] But to say that a man exists in a better way than a brute does is to attribute to them a real relation of similarity in existing. Although it is easy to see that in this relation the subject and the term are the man and the brute, it is not so easy to see what the foundation might be. For the foundation in this evaluation must account for the similarity between a human entitative act and a brute perfection of existing. And this is exactly the question at hand. Hence the first topic of this study may be phrased in another way. What is the foundation for the real relation of similarity-in-existing between a man and a brute?

The method of research that will yield a satisfactory answer to these ontological questions can only be a reflection on my own knowledge of being. Since being is intelligible, if all the possible solutions (1. essence of a limited being, 2. human *esse*, 3. human *esse* and brute *esse*, taken together, 4. the sum total of degrees of existing), which are furnished by limited beings, are discovered to be unsatisfactory because they involve a contradiction, it follows that Unlimited Being will remain as the adequate explanation. This reflection, at this point, will consider the following topics: Inadequate Solutions, the Adequate Solution, and a Demonstration.

INADEQUATE SOLUTIONS

The first solution suggested, the essence of a finite being, either of man or of brute, disqualifies as the ground for the parity between the variegated grades of existing in man and in an animal because such an essence is a passive potency in the order of existing, a capacity for receiving an act of existing. And to affirm that the ability to receive an act of existing is a sufficient reason for the resemblance between these existential perfections is to say that passive potency, the *limiting* principle, explains act, which is the *perfecting* principle. This would be a contradiction.

The human *esse*, the second solution proposed, also fails to meet the criterion of intelligibility. Of course, the human entitative act, insofar as it ontologically excels the brute act of existing, explains why the former differs from the latter. But to employ the human perfection of existing also to account for their likeness is to claim that the human *esse* and the brute *esse* differ and are similar under the same respect, which is again a contradiction. In like manner, no Aristotelian would write that two men differ and are alike due to prime matter, an intrinsic potential principle in every human essence. It would be unthinkable for the judge in a music festival, after declaring one tenor's rendition of the Toreador song more perfect than that of another contestant's, to decide that the two vocalists tied for first place since their achievements were so similar.

In the third place, neither will the human existential perfection and the brute existential act taken together do as the ultimate basis for their mutual similarity. Again, because man's act of existing is a higher ontological value than a brute's perfection of existing, evidently both existential degrees taken together ground their reciprocal difference. However, to base this difference and this similarity on these entitative acts taken together is to state that they differ and are similar according to the same respect, which is another contradiction.

Yet it is otherwise when measuring a yardstick and a one-foot ruler against each other. They are alike and different according to their dimensions, without implying a contradiction. While they correspond perfectly for twelve inches, the additional twenty-four inches in the longer measure differ completely from the absence of any quantity beyond one foot in the smaller ruler.

Fourthly, the sum total of degrees of existing is of no help in resolving the problem. As it is itself a degree of existing, the sum total of grades of existing is subject to the same difficulty that besets the human entitative act as the explanatory principle of the resemblance under investigation. Whereas the existential act of man and the existential act of an animal differ mutually due to these acts themselves, the reason for their mutual similarity is not the sum total of the degrees of existence, because the degrees intervening between an animal act of existing and the sum total of the degrees differ from the grades ranging between a human act of existing and the sum total of the grades.

An example brings out the point here. After three art students have each painted a copy of the original Mona Lisa, suppose the instructor assigns grades of seventy, eighty, ninety to the student paintings. Surely the pictures that receive the two lowest grades differ from each other. Yet no one would claim that the reason for their mutual similarity is the remaining student painting, since obviously the numerical value between seventy and ninety is greater than between seventy and eighty.

ADEQUATE SOLUTION

With all the possible explanations from finite beings investigated and found unsatisfactory, and granting that being is intelligible, the question is finally answered by Unlimited Being. The affirmation that there is an act of existing without limit, the act of existing beyond the degrees in its infinite perfection, the perfection of existing containing in itself the whole perfection of existing — this is the ultimate reason for the likeness between man's existence and a brute's existence. While these degrees differ and are many, due to their differing grades of existing, they are similar and are one on account of Pure *Esse*, which is imitated by each degree albeit differently. In other words, the infinite entitative act (the exemplar) – which is resembled in different ways by the differing grades of existing (the exemplates) – is the correct foundation for the real relation of similarity between man's perfection of existing and a brute's existential act. Thus the different degrees of existing resemble each other because they all resemble the unlimited act of existing.

An example from art parallels this solution. Just as two paintings of the Mona Lisa awarded different grades by an art teacher are similar insofar as they both imitate the original picture, which is beyond grading, so a man's act of existing and an animal's act of existing are alike because they imitate Infinite *Esse*, which is beyond the degrees. Of course, this is only an analogy. It is with the eye of the body that one sees the copies and the original painting. But it is only with the eye of the mind that one affirms the act of existing in limited beings, i.e., the effect and the truth of the proposition that there is pure act of existing, the First Exemplary Cause.

A DEMONSTRATION

The entire preceding analysis can be epitomized in a syllogism demonstrating the existence of God from the different degrees of existing. First step: A human act of existing is superior to a brute act of existing. Second step: But superiority is affirmed of a human *esse* in comparison with a brute *esse* since they both imitate differently the infinite act of existing. Conclusion: Therefore there is an infinite act of existing.

The evidence for the premises of this argument has already been presented in the first part of this chapter. As confirmation of this evidence, consider that the human *esse* and the brute *esse* are degrees, not of human existence, not of human and brute existence taken together, not of the sum total of the existential grades, but of the act of existing itself.

Since the structured proof above is a particularization of Aquinas' argument of the Fourth Way, Thomas' text is given here.

..."The fourth way is taken from degrees which are found in things. For in things there is found something more and less good, and true, and noble: and this is so with other perfections of this kind. But more and less are said of different things according as they approach, in different ways, something which is the highest: as a thing is hotter the more it approaches the hottest. Therefore, there is something which is truest and best, and noblest, and, consequently, the highest being. For those things which are the highest in truth are the highest in being, as Aristotle says in Book II of the *Metaphysics*."[4]

PART AND GRADE

Just as a comparison of a real relation of quantity with a real relation of similarity between different degrees of existential acts assisted us in the elaboration of the previous inquiry, so a contrast of a part of quantity with a degree of the entitative act will be the second means of elucidating the Fourth Way dialectic. Hence the differences between part and grade, described by the late Rev. Aloisius Korinek, S.J.,[5] in his recently privately printed book on natural theology, will disclose the meaning of a perfection which is used in the Fourth Way, i.e., one whose notion contains no imperfection. His ensemble of the Six Ways, in which a part and a grade differ, will be explained now.

First of all, the quantitative aspect of beings, but not their entitative aspect, can be added together. A yardstick can be assembled by joining a twelve-inch ruler with a twenty-four inch measure. But a brute act of existing does not result from splicing together a plant act of existing with another act of existing.[6]

Secondly, adjectives appropriately modifying the perfection of quantity are not the same as those adequately describing the perfection of being. A yardstick is not qualitatively better than but quantitatively bigger than a one-foot ruler; whereas brute existence is not quantitatively bigger than but qualitatively better than plant existence.[7]

Thirdly, divisibility applies to a body possessing quantity, a lateral perfection found in all material things, but not to the act of existing, a vertical perfection present in all beings. Thus a yardstick is a quantified body with potential parts. But the entitative act of a brute is a simple quality without parts.[8]

Fourthly, the word "part" applies to a quantified object while the word "degree" or "grade" fits the qualitative perfection of being. For example, a yardstick is a part of quantity. On the other hand, a brute act of being is a degree or grade of *esse*.[9]

Fifthly, our way of knowing the foundation of a real relation of quantity differs from our way of knowing the foundation of a real relation of similarity in existing. The act of comparing two quantified objects includes explicit knowledge of quantity before further analysis leads to the explicit affirmation of quantity as the foundation for the comparison. This prior explicit knowledge is both sensation of extension or quantity (as a common sensible object) and intellectual apprehension (objectively representing these dimensions or quantity).

On the other hand, affirming the similarity between different grades of entitative act contains no explicit but only implicit knowledge of maximal being, before further examination yields a demonstration which concludes with the explicit affirmation of the infinite ontological act as the foundation for the likeness. There is no prior explicit knowledge of Pure *Esse* because neither sensing, nor intellectual apprehending, nor existential affirming attain the pure act of existing. There is no sensation of Infinite *Esse* because both the proper sensible objects, what can be known by only one sense power, and the common sensible objects, what can be known by more than one sense power (but only through a proper sensible object), do not embrace existence. Neither is there apprehension of the unlimited act of existing since material essence, the object of the first act of the mind, is not the act of existing. Nor, finally, is there existential affirmation of the infinite act of existing. The reason is that the act of existing of a material being, the object of the existential judgment, is not Pure *Esse*.

An example summarizes this absence of explicit knowledge of the highest being. A student once said, "I don't hear existence." To be more complete he should have said, "I don't sense, nor apprehend, but I do existentially affirm the act of existing of a limited, material being.[10] But I neither sense, nor apprehend, nor existentially judge Pure *Esse*." However, according to Korinek, the act of affirming that different degrees of existing are alike does involve implicit knowledge of Pure *Esse*.

What is this implicit knowledge? Since being is intelligible, what ultimately explains the similarity between human *esse* and brute *esse* is also intelligible.[11] In my initial question, I knew there was an answer although I did not know what the answer was. At that time, I had implicit knowledge of the solution, Pure *Esse*.

Similarly, since scientists can discover remedies for diseases, Dr. Jonas Salk knew that the remedy for polio could be detected. In his preliminary investigation he knew there was an answer, even though he did not know what the answer was. Then he had implicit knowledge of the vaccine that would be a remedy for polio. After I concluded that Pure *Esse* grounds the similarity between human *esse* and brute *esse*, I explicitly knew the solution to my problem.[12] Likewise, upon discovering the cure for polio, Dr. Salk explicitly knew the vaccine that is the remedy for polio.

Of course, this is only an analogy. For one thing, the outcome of the demonstration of God's existence is a proposition known to be true because of evidence given in the Fourth Way.[13] The experiments of the scientist, however, resulted in the discovery of a vaccine, which can be verified by controlled sensory observation.

Sixthly and finally, a direct mutual comparison of two bodies differing in size warrants judging that one is longer than the other; but an indirect comparison of different entitative degrees with the infinite act of existing is the basis for recognizing, during the first step of the fourth proof, the similarity between these different grades of existing.

On the one hand, direct measuring of a yardstick and a one-foot ruler by each other is possible because the intellect, throughout the entire process of measuring, explicitly knows the univocal quantity which is common to both items used.

On the other hand, while direct reciprocal measuring of human *esse* and brute *esse* is impossible since the act of existing is an analogous perfection intrinsic to man and brute, the indirect comparing of these different existential degrees with maximal being in the initial phase of the Fourth Way is possible because the intellect in the early stage of the argument has implicit knowledge of maximal being. In brief, this indirect comparison means that my affirmations of human *esse* and brute *esse* include implicit knowledge of Pure *Esse*. I have described previously how this implicit knowledge occurs.

Perhaps Korinek's notion of indirect comparison may furnish another view of how absolute being grounds the similarity between different entitative acts. Might not the intellect, reflecting on the first step in the Fourth Way, consider that the proximate reason for the similarity between two different degrees of existing is that both the affirmation of an inferior degree of being and the affirmation of a superior degree of being fail to answer the intellect's query about the similarity between the different degrees of existing.

And might not the intellect scrutinizing the second step in the Fourth Way recognize that the ultimate reason for the likeness between various grades of existing is that affirming the truth of the plentitude of being, which is imitated by all the degrees, does answer the intellect's inquiry concerning the similarity between different grades of existing.

Thus the outer approach to the absolute, developed in the first part of this chapter, goes hand in hand with the inner path to God described in Korinek's theory of indirect comparison. Stated in another way, different degrees of existence imitating absolute being is duplicated by the human intellect's discovery that the question about the similarity between different degrees of existing is answered by affirming there is Pure *Esse*.[14]

With this dual explanation, the Fourth Way avoids begging the question.[15] Such a fallacy would be committed were explicit knowledge of maximal being claimed in the initial step of the Fourth Way. It is avoided, however, because the argument asserts only implicit knowledge of the supreme being in the first part of the demonstration.

In recapitulation of the contrasts between a grade of the act of existing and a part of quantity, six characteristics of the perfection of existing are specified by Korinek. The act of existing of a superior finite being does not result from adding together the acts of existing of two inferior beings, but is qualitatively better than the perfection of existing of a lower being, is a simple quality without parts and is called a degree of existing. Affirming the act of existing of a being of experience includes implicit knowledge of maximal being; the Fourth Way concludes to explicit knowledge of the truth of the unlimited act of existing. In the first stage of the Fourth Way, affirming that different grades of existing are similar, involves an indirect comparison of these degrees with maximal being implicitly affirmed in every affirmation of a degree of being.

AN OBJECTION

Although objections to understanding the Fourth Way are as numerous as the difficulties of walking through thorny underbrush, the final method of clarification used in this essay will propose only one objection because the two parts of Aquinas' text on the fourth proof provide the basis for a double answer to the difficulty. A student once expressed this same objection at the end of his seminar report on the proof of God from the degrees of perfection. "The failure of the Fourth Way," he commented, "to account for the essences of graded beings is the only difficulty preventing me from assigning certitude to the conclusion of the Fourth Way." As the first part of Thomas' text concerning the fourth argument has already been cited in this study, only the second part of this quotation is now reproduced.

"Now what is stated as the highest in some genus, is the cause of all in that genus: as fire, which is the highest heat, is the cause of all hot things, as is said in the same book. Therefore, there is something which for all beings is the cause of *esse*, of goodness, and other perfections of this kind: and this we call God."[16]

How, then, does the bi-partite structure of the text containing the Fourth Way dissolve the difficulty? The two parts of the passage correspond to the two stages in the resolution of the objection. The purpose of the first part of the text is to ascend from the affirmation of the degrees of existing to the affirmation that there is the maximal being, the exemplary cause of all graded beings. Since this procedure constitutes a proof (for God) whose scope is to explain the similarity of the different notes on the scale of existence in limited beings, failure to explain the essence of these beings is not a deficiency in the argument. This is the first stage of the reply to the difficulty previously proposed.

As L. Charlier[17] in his recent article on the Five Ways

maintains that the second part of the text under discussion deals with the procession of creatures from God, from the First Efficient Cause, his analysis of this part of the passage explicitly treats the origin of the essence of a limited being. Therefore, according to him, the intent of the second part of the text is to descend from affirming that there is the highest degree of being, the First Efficient Cause of the degrees, to affirming the degrees of being.

How does he understand this efficient causality? It has three aspects. First of all, maximal being, the effficient cause, grounds the similarity between graded beings and itself. In the words of Aquinas, "For since every agent reproduces its like so far as it is an agent, and everything acts in accord with its form, the effect must in some way resemble the form of the agent. [...] In this way all created things, so far as they are beings, are likened to God, as the first and universal Source of all existence."[18]

Secondly, the highest degree, efficient cause, guarantees the act of existence of graded beings. God's efficient causality must not be conceived quantitatively as if God loses parts of His own act of existing by placing particles of the act of existing "outside Himself" as creatures.[19] Rather, the highest degree of the act of existing is qualitatively "present to all the degrees by imparting itself to them without division or loss to itself."[20]

A good example of this communication of existence is to be found in a speaker's presentation of thought to an audience. When Robert Frost explained his poem *The Hired Man* to an audience of a thousand persons, he did not lose parts of his own knowledge by giving each member of the audience a particle of knowledge, as a waiter distributes after-dinner drinks. Rather, Frost's thought was qualitatively present to all the listeners by the entire discourse being spoken to all at the same time, without division of or loss to the speaker's knowledge.

Here is another example. In striking language the late Rev. Gerald Phelan used to tell his students that God is Phelan in the sense that whatever perfection of existence Phelan has, God "already" is; moreover, he taught that

Phelan is not God because whatever of limitation or essence there be in Phelan, God is not.[21]

To express the communication of existence still another way, limited being constantly borrows its being from God, surely not separated but distinct from the divine being, however totally dependent on infinite being, its source. In other words, my *esse* is not separated from Pure *Esse* because *esse* is an indivisible simple quality. However, my *esse* is really distinct from Pure *Esse* due to my essence, a potential component, limiting intrinsically my *esse*, an actual component. Nevertheless both components are continually sustained by Pure *Esse*.

Thirdly, the supreme being, efficient cause, establishes the multiplicity of the beings in the degrees. Multiple beings are each composed of intrinsic principles of being, essence and the act of existing, which are related as potency and act. The potential component, essence, which limits its correlative act of existing, accounts for the multiplicity of participated beings. God, the supreme principle of graded beings, creates the essence of such beings with the existence.

"God at the same time gives *esse* and produces that which receives *esse*."[22]

This explanation of the origin of the essences of limited beings is the second stage of the response to the initial objection that the Fourth Way fails to take into account the essences of graded beings.

How the two parts of the text correlate with the two phases, in the dissolution of the difficulty first proposed, may now be summarized. Although the first part, which delineates the Fourth Way, accounts not for the essences of limited beings but for the similarity between different degrees of entitative acts by affirming that there is the infinite act of existing, the second part, which identifies maximal being with the First Efficient Cause, implies that both the essence and the *esse* of limited beings take their origin from Pure *Esse*. Thus, it is true that the Fourth Way itself does not consider the essence of a limited being; but the second part of the text does take up the essence of a limited being by implying that such an essence proceeds from Pure *Esse*.

To state the connection between the two parts of the above text in another manner, exemplary causality, expressed in the first part of the text, is connected with efficient causality, designated in the second part of the text. Accordingly, both parts of the text can be explained as follows. God knowing His own Productive Idea, the Exemplar, the Model, Pure *Esse*, continually efficiently creates the human *esse* with its essence and the brute *esse* with its essence so that both degrees of *esse* are similar in so far as they both imitate Pure *Esse*. To refer to the example given before, the two art students — according to their own productive ideas, the exemplars, the models, their own ideas of the Mona Lisa — apply brush and paint to pieces of canvas in order that both finished paintings might be similar in as much as they both imitate the Mona Lisa. Briefly, in the above bi-partite text, exemplary causality is linked with efficient causality.

CONCLUSION

Has this chapter succeeded in clarifying the Fourth Way? Comparing three recent interpretations of the fourth proof with the position presented in this essay may help answer this question. Although all four writers seek to ground the principle of exemplary causality, namely that different degrees of existing are affirmed insofar as they imitate differently the unlimited act of existing, they explain that ground differently.

The first author[23] claims that the principle of exemplary causality is true because

> "*the source of the intelligibility of these minorated degrees of the same perfection [can be...] only the existence of the unlimited, unreceived degree.*"

The second philosopher[24] expresses the evidence for the principle of exemplarity as follows.

> "If that which is in the highest degree were not existing,
> if it were pure creation of my intellect, I would find
> myself with this inexplicable and contradictory fact: [...]
> a perfection which of itself does not admit limit and
> which does not exist in itself is found among things
> graded and limited."

The third writer[25] says the basis for the exemplary
proposition is that

> "this absolute [explains...] why one and the same value
> could be found more or less diminished in existents of
> lesser perfection."

This present essay grounds the exemplary causal
proposition in this way. Affirming the truth of the plentitude
of being, the exemplar, both being imitated differently by
all the degrees of existing and completely answering the
question of my intellect, ultimately accounts for the
similarity between the different grades of existing. In view
of these four explanations, it does seem that this present
quest has made the Fourth Way more understandable
without claiming, of course, to solve completely the mystery
of being.

The approach to God described in this study has other
results. It reveals the total grandeur of finite beings mirror-
ing, reflecting and imitating Pure *Esse*. It may serve as a
philosophical basis for the poet's claim to find God in all
things.

> "There was a time when meadow, grove and stream,
> The earth and every common sight,
> To me did seem
> Apparelled in celestial light."[26]

And it may provide a fundamental ingredient for a
philosophy of society befitting the dignity of the human
person in which priority is given to quality over quantity,

to work over money, to the human over the technological, to wisdom over science, to the service of humanity over the unlimited aggrandizement of the individual or of the State.[27]

A CONTEM-PORARY APPROACH

A CONTEMPORARY APPROACH
TO GOD'S EXISTENCE

L et us start with a parable. On one occasion, a full moon shining through the window of a faculty lounge prompted an astronomer and a metaphysician to discuss the discoveries of the space age. The scientist said, "We now know as a scientific fact that the distance between the moon and the earth is two hundred thirty-nine thousand miles on an average since the orbit of the moon is not a perfect circle." "How do we have such exact knowledge?" the other inquired. The scientist explained the use of the laser beam in computing the precise number of miles from the earth. Then the conversation turned to philosophy with the metaphysician's observation, "The activity itself of knowing the scientific fact about the moon being so many miles from the earth can be the starting point in demon-strating the existence of God."[1] "How can this be done?" the astronomer wondered.

This parable introduces the subject under investigation in this chapter. Note that the question is not whether a scientific fact may be the first step in establishing the existence of God. Rather, the issue is whether knowing the scientific fact can be the initial phase in reasoning to God's existence. In keeping with the parable, I shall attempt to answer this question in a way that can be followed by a scientist unfamiliar with philosophical argument.

Demonstrating God's existence from knowing a scientific fact requires the cooperative effort of a scientist and a philosopher. The scientist, by furnishing a *scientific* fact to be known, provides the first stage of the argument, and the philosopher, by presenting a *metaphysical* elucidation of this initial step, contributes the remaining stages of the reasoning process. With a scientific fact already given by the astronomer in the above parable, the philosophical analysis will proceed as follows: an analysis of knowing a scientific fact, examination of this analysis, no first cause, first cause, a comparison, and conclusion.

AN ANALYSIS OF KNOWING A SCIENTIFIC FACT

Of the many aspects involved in knowing the distance between the moon and the earth, only one will be examined in this study. Anyone knowing this scientific fact will grant that there are at least three aspects of this conscious activity: the objects known, such as the moon and the earth, the human knower, and the act of knowing itself. This analysis will not be pointed toward the objects known, nor toward the subject knowing, but toward the act of scientific knowing. This is to scrutinize the very mystery of human cognitional activity.[2] I will not give an exhaustive account of human knowing, but merely study the act of knowing the scientific fact.

The cognition of the scientific fact about the mileage between the moon and the earth is not an object of sense knowledge. The object of sensory knowledge includes both the six proper sensible objects (color, sound, odor, flavor, temperature, resistance) and the five common sensible objects (extension, motion, rest, shape, and number). All who internally examine their own act of knowing how far the moon is from the earth will admit readily that this cognitive activity is not the pale yellow color of the moon on a clear evening, nor is it sound, odor, flavor, hot or cold, rough or smooth. The same analysis applies to the common sensible objects. All who study their own cognition of the scientific fact given above will surely grant that this cognitive act is not spherical in shape like a full moon, nor is it extended, in motion, at rest, a number. The cognitional act being investigated is simply beyond the object of sensory knowing. In brief, this act of cognition is not an object of sense experience, i.e., an object of external and internal sensation.[3]

Another example of an act of knowing which is not observable by the senses may help here. Although I am aware of my own conscience informing me that to take a magazine from a store rack without paying for it must not be done, this directive given by my conscience is not visible to someone else, nor do I see the conscience internally guiding another person.[4]

Recently, philosophers have emphasized that human knowing activity is not a phenomenon to be investigated by the procedures used in the natural sciences. Rev. Martin C. D'Arcy, S.J., quotes Dr. Ropp's warning that "the scientist who attempts to study the chemistry of thought... resembles a burglar attempting to open a vault of one of the world's largest banks with a toothpick."[5] Eric Mascall, noting that a calculating machine cannot be intelligently self-conscious, rules out "variables in any physical equation which stand for conscious states or activities."[6]

Further analysis reveals that the act of knowing a scientific fact is neither *making* something nor *receiving* something.[7] Knowing the earth, the moon, and the distance between them is not the same as producing a work of art from existing material, like Rodin carving the statue of Balzac out of stone. Consequently, a knower in knowing a scientific fact does not change the object known, whereas the artist in creating an art object in some way changes the material used in the process. Cognition about the number of miles between the moon and the earth is different from receiving food. Thus, someone knowing a scientific fact does not destroy the object known, whereas an animal eating food destroys the object eaten. Therefore, in cognitive activity, the known object is neither changed nor destroyed.

Viewed positively, knowing that the moon is two hundred thirty-nine thousand miles from the earth is an existence.[8] First, when I have cognition that the moon is so many miles from the earth, I am aware of the moon, the earth, and the distance between them, i.e., I am present to this scientific fact. Therefore, to know the object in question is to be aware of that object. Secondly, when I come to know that the moon is so far from the earth, I am united with the moon, the earth, and the mileage between them. Hence, knowing the object being studied is in some way a union between the subject and that object. Thirdly, when I have knowledge of the exact expanse between the moon and the earth, in a certain sense, I am the moon, the earth, and the intervening number of miles. It follows that knowing the object is for the knower to be that object. In sum, cognitive activity is to be aware of a scientific fact, a union between the knower and that scientific fact – i.e., simply an existence. If I let a pencil fall from my hand to the top of a desk, I am aware of a falling object; there is a union between me and the moving object; in a sense I am the changing object.

Further analysis discloses that to know a scientific fact is a superexistence. For there is a difference between a human person merely existing and the same person existing as knowing the space mileage between the moon and the earth. In the former case, I shall call existing substantial *esse*, the *esse* that actuates essence. In the latter case, again I shall name existing substantial *esse* but I shall assign to knowing a scientific fact a better act of existing,[9] an intentional *esse*, a cognitional existence, a superexistence. To put it another way, knowing a scientific fact is novelty in existence in comparison with the act of existing by which a human person is. Hence knowing a scientific fact is aptly called a superexistence. In brief, superexistence means that to know is to be the other as other not by substantial *esse*.

Thus far I have established the following: A cognitive act is not an object of external or internal sensation; it neither changes nor destroys the object known; such knowing is to be aware of an object, a union between knower and known, an act of existing, even a superexistence.[10]

EXAMINATION OF THIS ANALYSIS

What type of cognition is employed when I proceed from being aware of how far the moon is from the earth to knowing the intentional *esse* of my cognition about this distance? In other words, from an initial stage of knowing a certain scientific fact, there is a transition to knowing the cognitional *esse* of that knowing; I inquire neither about cognition in the initial stage nor about cognition in the final stage, but about naming the method of cognition conducting me throughout all three aspects of this cognitional transition: the start, the change, and the result.

My search will consist in considering which one of the following three knowledge methods is most adequate. These ways of knowing are direct knowledge, reflexive knowledge, and introspective knowledge.

Direct knowledge disqualifies because it is too narrow in scope to cover the transition from cognition of the scientific fact to knowing the *esse* of that cognition.

Witnessing that the sun warms the stone,[11] an instance of direct knowing, is knowledge of an object that is beyond what is knowable by the external senses and includes what can be known by these senses. The connection between the sun and the stone is neither a proper nor common sensible object, and, hence, is not known by the external senses, whereas the color of the sun and the warmth of the stone can be known by the senses. Therefore, direct knowledge, according to the point of view taken in this study, is cognition of an object, some of whose components are knowable by the external senses.[12]

When I apply this type of knowledge to the cognitional transition being discussed, direct cognition clearly applies to the initial stage, namely, knowing that two hundred thirty-nine thousand miles intervene between moon and earth; but not to the last stage, namely, knowing the intentional *esse* of direct cognition. For, in the first stage by direct cognition, the intellect knows the exact distance between the moon and the earth, and the senses know the color and shape of the moon. But, in the final stage by direct cognition, I do not know the existence of cognition about this scientific fact, simply because intentional *esse* is not sensible.

Reflexive knowledge also is not an apt vehicle for describing the cognitive transition from cognition of a scientific fact to cognition of the existence of that knowledge. However, it is not as easy to rule out reflexive knowledge as it is to rule out direct knowledge. For one thing, different philosophers define reflexive knowledge differently. The difficulty diminishes, however, if I restrict reflexive knowledge to mean inadvertent knowing of direct cognition, adding that I inadvertently know in the very act by which I directly know. To put it another way, direct cognition is a double awareness: awareness of an object, some of whose components can be known by the external senses, and inadvertent awareness of the direct cognition itself.[13] This latter awareness is what I mean by reflexive knowledge.

Suppose I ask a spectator in a theatre during a performance of Shakespeare's King Lear two questions. "Are you aware that you are knowing the plot of the drama as it unfolds? Before you were asked, were you deliberately adverting to the fact that you are aware of this knowledge?" No doubt, the first question would receive an affirmative reply, and the second question would be answered negatively. In the latter case, the spectator's inadvertent awareness of his own knowledge of the stage play being enacted is an instance of reflexive knowledge.

A comparison of reflexive cognition and the cognitive change being considered reveals that reflexive knowledge corresponds with the initial stage of the intentional change but not with the final stage. Reflexive cognition is certainly another facet of the starting point, i.e., direct knowledge of the distance intervening between the moon and the earth, since by reflexive knowledge I am inadvertently aware of this direct cognition in the very act by which

I know the scientific fact. However, reflexive knowledge does not extend to the result of the cognitive transition that concerns me: knowing the *esse* of directly knowing a scientific fact. The reason is that reflexive cognition, a component of direct cognition, precedes the philosophical analysis in which I know the intentional *esse* of direct cognition. Of course, if I ask my imaginary theatre patron a final question, "Are you aware that you are knowing the super-existence of knowing the dramatic plot?" the answer surely will be negative.

Introspective knowledge, finally, is a suitable instrument for embracing all three stages of the cognitive transition that interests me. As with reflexive knowledge, thinkers do not define the act of introspecting exactly the same way.[14] Once again, as with reflexive knowledge, I shall confine introspective knowledge to signify a deliberate turning from direct cognition to knowing a characteristic of that cognition.[15]

The three stages of introspective knowledge – the direct cognition, the deliberate turning,[16] and knowing an aspect of direct knowing – can be verified easily in the following example. Upon being questioned, a student will admit readily that the desk in front of the room is heavier and longer than a pencil in the instructor's hand. This, of course, provides an instance of direct cognition. And, it will be at the urging of the teacher that the student will turn deliberately from a direct cognition about a quantitative comparison to answer an inquiry concerning a characteristic of that direct knowledge. Upon further questioning, the student also will grant that his act of knowing about the desk being heavier and longer than the pencil is itself without weight and size. Thus, the student knows an aspect of his own direct cognition.

Measuring the above tripartite definition of introspection by the three moments of the cognitional motion that concerns me manifests that the former admirably conforms to the latter. Indeed, knowing the exact intervening distance between the moon and the earth is an illustration of direct cognition. The passage itself from knowing the scientific fact to knowing the existence of that knowing is certainly a deliberate transition. Lastly, knowing the superexistence of that space knowledge is an aspect of the original direct cognition. In retrospect, passing from direct cognition of a scientific fact to an awareness of the intentional *esse* of that cognition is not direct knowledge, nor reflexive knowledge, but introspective knowledge.

The work of classifying the cognitive processes serving thus far in my demonstration of God's existence would be incomplete if, at this point, I did not indicate that both direct cognition of exactly how far the moon is from the earth as well as knowing the existence of that cognition are acts of thinking or of intellection. By now it is easy to establish that directly knowing the scientific fact mentioned is an act of thinking by noticing that this direct cognition is at the same time reflexive knowledge, which cannot be said of an act of sensation like seeing the white color of this page.[17] No one would admit seeing an act of seeing the white color of this paper. And so, seeing is not simultaneously reflexive cognition. On the other hand, knowing the *esse* of the direct awareness of the same scientific fact is an act of intellection, since sensation always attains a proper sensible object, and the intentional existence of direct cognition is beyond all the proper sensible objects. In other words, reflexive knowledge and knowing *esse*, two kinds of cognition not found in sensation, are verified in a direct cognitional act and in knowing the existence of that cognition respectively. Thus an act of direct cognition and knowing the *esse* of direct knowledge are better acts of knowing than sensation. I name these better cognitive acts thinking or intellection.[18] To sum up, my demonstration, then, begins with two acts of intellection: *direct* thinking (about a certain scientific fact) evolving into *introspective* thinking (about the existence of that direct thinking).

No First Cause

The central question in my enterprise of demonstrating God's existence concerns not the first stage in the procedure:

directly thinking about the two hundred thirty-nine thousand miles between the moon and the earth. It rather concerns the second stage: introspecting the *esse* of the previous direct intellection. Does the existence of thinking about this scientific fact depend ultimately on Absolute Existence?[19] Can the intentional *esse* of intellectually knowing the length of a journey between the earth and the moon be fully explained only by Pure *Esse*? Is the super*esse* of direct intellection about this scientific fact ultimately grounded only in Absolute *Esse*?

Whoever considers why four philosophers would respond negatively to the central question just formulated will be better prepared to understand why a realist answers this key question affirmatively.[20] This would be especially true of someone unacquainted with philosophical thinking, like the astronomer in the parable at the beginning of this study. For this reason, I now explain briefly why Plato, Kant, a Positivist, and Nagel would not admit that I can know the ultimate dependence of intentional *esse* on the actual influence of Pure *Esse*. (No one is denying, of course, that these thinkers have contributed substantially to our understanding of ourselves and our environment. But with regard to accounting for cognitional existence, they are mute.)

Plato's philosophy can't deal with the question about the ultimate ground of intentional *esse* because Platonism is a philosophy of essences. In his famous dialogues Plato, in order to establish that true reality is a world of Separated Ideas, Forms, or Essences, applied a presupposition from Parmenides to definitions. What is *thought* is what *is*, Parmenides had said. Since "what is thought" is a concept and "what is" is reality, Plato concluded that concept, or definition, corresponds perfectly with reality. Noticing that any definition, like that of a triangle, is immaterial, immutable, infinite, necessary, and universal, Plato used the correspondence principle to argue that true reality, such as the reality of a triangle, is likewise immaterial, immutable, infinite, necessary, and universal. This reality is a Separated Idea, Form, or Essence. In the *Republic*, Plato wrote that we assume an Idea whenever we apply the same name to many separate things.[21] However, this entire procedure applies only to essence, since a definition is the mental expression of an essence, and the Separated Idea is also an Essence. Intentional existence is not an essence and therefore is excluded from the Platonic analysis.

Among other reasons, Kant's notion of being makes it impossible for his philosophy to account for the ultimate cause of intentional being. What is his notion of being? *Being*, he said, is not a real predicate,[22] a synthetic predicate, one that not only adds to the subject, but also enlarges it.[23] For instance, "warms" is such a predicate in the proposition "The sun warms the stone."[24] Rather, *being* is either a category or experience. As a category, "being" is a copula, a logical predicate, one that adds nothing to the subject but merely posits the subject and all its predicates as in the proposition, "A triangle is a three-angled figure."[25] In the proposition just given, "is" signifies "is as a category." "Being as experience," however, does not enlarge the subject, but does add an additional possible perception.[26] Now an actual perception for Kant is an appearance combined with consciousness.[27] And appearance is a synthesis of sensation-in-general and the sense forms of space and time.[28] In the following example given by Kant, "real" refers to something that "exists as experience." "My financial condition is affected differently by a hundred real dollars than it is by a hundred possible dollars."[29]

From this explanation, it follows that neither "is as a category" nor "exists as experience" has the same meaning as intentional existence. The function of "is as a category" is to connect the subject and the predicate in an analytic proposition, while intentional *esse* describes the thinking activity itself. "Exists as experience", however, adds sensation to space as in the example "a body is heavy." But the intentional act of existing, as explained before, is in no way sensible. Therefore intentional *esse* is outside the notion of being presented in the *Critique of Pure Reason*. And this Kantian notion, accordingly, cannot help in discovering the ultimate source of intentional *esse*.

Because of his view that the human mind is open only to one level of truth, that is, the realm of knowledge based on scientific facts, a Positivist is of no assistance in the search for the ultimate ground of intentional being. Why would a Positivist deny plural levels of truth? One explanation is that he or she has pursued research into scientific facts, i.e., facts established immediately or mediately by scientific observation,[30] so exclusively that one is closed to any other level of truth.[31]

Be that as it may, a Positivist would maintain consistently that questions about another level of truth, philosophical facts, i.e., facts arising from a philosophical analysis of experience, like the existence of motion, the existence of things, the existence of thought,[32] are meaningless. And so, intentional *esse*, not a scientific fact but a philosophical fact, has no meaning for a Positivist. Here I certainly do not condemn a scientist who refuses to exchange the scientist's cap for the philosopher's cap and ask a philosophical question. But I do have misgivings about any thinker who will not allow the human mind to search for the answer to a philosophical question.[33]

With empirical evidence supporting his double-level theory of reality, Ernest Nagel constructs a philosophy of naturalism[34] in which the question about whether Absolute Existence ultimately grounds intentional existence is without meaning. He opts for the empirical method since it seems to be the most reliable way of knowing there is.[35] Moreover, naturalism maintains that reality is twofold, including not only material bodies and organizations of material bodies but also what is beyond these bodies and their organizations, namely, forms of behavior and functions of material systems such as modes of action, plans, aspirations. But, although forms and functions are parts of nature, they are not agents that bring themselves or others into concrete reality.[36] Thus naturalism has no room for an immaterial mind guiding the course of events.[37] Since cognitional existence cannot be classified as a material system, naturalism has no room for it either.

FIRST CAUSE

A scientist, uninitiated in the ways of philosophy, wondering about whether intentional *esse* depends on the actual influence of Absolute *Esse*, noticing the reasons why Platonism, Kantianism, positivism, and naturalism cannot deal with the question, might be inclined to consider why realism claims to answer this pivotal question. To serve this purpose, a realist might propose the following argument by exclusion. Either intentional existence has no sufficient reason, or it is completely explained by the essence of the human being exercising this intentional act of existing, or it is fully accounted for by the substantial *esse* of the human person performing this intellectual activity, or it is ultimately grounded by the sum total of all the degrees of existing, the degrees of existing possessed by all finite beings, or it is fully intelligible by Pure *Esse*. Since being is intelligible, and since the above disjunction is complete, if the first four members of the disjunction are found to be unintelligible, Unlimited *Esse* will be the correct answer to the question.

Let us analyse the wrong solutions first. Of course, the first solution, the attempt to ground the intentional act of existing in no sufficient reason, is unacceptable because, for a realist, being is intelligible. Considering this initial solution to the question and its unsuitability reminds me that the principle of sufficient reason or intelligibility, not the principle of contradiction, is at the root of this demonstration of God's existence.[38]

The second answer has it that the essence of the human person who has the cognitional *esse* I am investigating, cannot account for this cognitional existence. Evidently, a human being is not identical with another existing rational animal. From this it follows that a human person does not contain the whole perfection of existing, but rather is deficient or limited in the perfection of being. Now the function of essence, an intrinsic principle of being, is precisely to explain this deficiency, this limitation in the perfection of being. In a phrase, essence in a human person is potency in the order of existing. And surely the effort to ground human intellection, a new perfection of existing, by the human essence, a potential principle, is clearly contradictory. It is germane here to note the realist's contention that I intellectually apprehend the essence of a human person while I intellectually affirm my own cognitional *esse*.

Thirdly, the substantial *esse* of a human person does not adequately explain the intentional *esse* exercised by that same person. Of course, the substantial act of existing and the intentional act of existing of a human subject are both similar and different. They are *similar* inasmuch as both are not complete beings but rather components of a human being, intrinsic principles of being, perfections in the reason of being. But they account for *different* perfections in a rational being. Substantial *esse* is the intrinsic component by which a human subject exists, while intentional *esse* is the intrinsic principle by which a human being is intentionally an object.

Now, measuring a person who merely exists by the same person existing with an intentional act of existing discredits the substantial *esse* as the total explanation of an intentional *esse* in the same individual. The reason is that an existing person who is intentionally an object exists in a better way than the same person merely existing. That is to say, a human being possessing substantial *esse* and cognitional *esse* exists in a better manner than the same being merely having substantial *esse*. So, a person existing as a thinking adult exists in a better degree than he did when he was a newly born infant. But to say that the substantial *esse* of a human person is the total reason of the intentional *esse* in that some being is to claim that an *inferior* degree of existing totally explains a *superior* degree of existing. This is unintelligible. An analogy may help here. A bean plant growing green leaves exists in a better way than the same plant living with white leaves. No botanist would claim that the plant itself is the total cause of the green color of the plant's leaves, since a plant grown entirely in a dark room develops white leaves. If it is placed in the sunlight the leaves begin turning green.

In the fourth place, the sum total of degrees of existing is not the ultimate ground for the intentional act of existing exercised by a human person whose substantial *esse*
is within the sum total of those degrees. The argument by
comparing degrees of existing also applies here. The sum
total of grades of existing and the intentional *esse* proceeding from a human person existing within the grades exist
in a better way than the same sum total of degrees without
that intentional *esse*. To insist that the sum total of the degrees of existing without intentional *esse* is the ultimate
ground for the sum total of degrees of being with the intentional act of being is to take the view that an inferior
degree of existing totally grounds a superior grade of being. Once again, this is not intelligible.

With the first four members of the complete disjunction discarded, and since I admit that there is a sufficient
reason for intentional *esse*, it follows that Pure *Esse* is this
sufficient reason. In other words, intentional existence does
depend on the actual influence of Pure Existence, the perfection of being beyond the grades in its infinite perfection,
the act of existing containing in itself the whole perfection
of existing, the First Efficient Cause.

Since the above disjunctive syllogism has provided
the last two stages in my proposed demonstration of God's
existence, all four stages of the complete argument can now
be assembled. First stage: I know that the moon is two hundred thirty-nine thousand miles from the earth, a scientific
fact. Second stage: the act of thinking this distance between
the moon and the earth is an intentional *esse*, which is a
philosophical fact known by introspective analysis. Third
stage: But this intentional act of existing ultimately depends
on the actual influence of Pure *Esse*, the First Efficient Cause.
Fourth stage: Therefore, this First Cause, Pure *Esse*, *is*. As I
have reasoned, the third stage, a causal proposition, has
been established by a disjunctive syllogism.

A COMPARISON

When I compare intentional *esse* and Pure *Esse*, additional features of the demonstration just completed appear. Intentional existence is a component, an intrinsic principle of a limited person; Pure Existence is being. In a human being, substantial *esse* and cognitional *esse* cannot be divided into two beings but nevertheless are really *distinct*; in God, substantial *esse* and intellection are *identical* because intellection is a superexistence while Pure *Esse*, as we have established, is Infinite, containing in itself the whole perfection of existing.[39] As I indicated above, intentional *esse* is not an object of sensory experience; nor is Absolute *Esse* an object of sense experience.[40] Rather, by using philosophical analysis, I introspect the existence of my own direct intellection. On the other hand, at the conclusion of my proof, I know that Pure *Esse is*, inasmuch as I affirm that the proposition "Absolute *Esse is*" is true. The evidence for this proposition is simply that Pure Existence is the ultimate ground for cognitional *esse*.[41] Finally, an intentional act of existing is an effect since it is a new perfection of existing in comparison with substantial *esse*; Pure *Esse* is the First Efficient Cause actually influencing through the human person, who is the secondary efficient cause, the cognitional existence of that person. Undoubtedly, the human knower is an efficient cause of his own cognition. After all, he is the one who is performing the act of knowing.[42]

How God and Man influence intentional *esse* is as mysterious as how God and man produce a human free act.[43] But Josef Pieper reminds me not to be dismayed at this. *Science*, he says, in principle can answer fully the questions it asks, while *philosophy* can never answer finally its questions.[44] The poet writes about this mysterious union of God and human knowledge.

> *"O Lord, you have probed me and you know me;*
> *you know when I sit and when I stand;*
> *You understand my thoughts from afar.*

> *My journeys and my rest you scrutinize,*
> *with all my ways you are familiar.*
> *Even before a word is on my tongue,*
> *behold, O Lord, you know the whole of it.*
> *Behind me and before me, you hem me in*
> *and rest your hand upon me.*
> *Such knowledge is too wonderful for me;*
> *too lofty for me to attain."*[45]

CONCLUSION

Is this chapter appropriately entitled "A Contemporary Approach to God's Existence?" It seems so for two reasons. In the first step of the proof, the use of the laser beam established the scientific fact about the exact distance between the moon and the earth. This fact, in turn, specified the direct act of thinking, which is the launching pad for this way to God. The second stage of the demonstration developed in this essay used the "turn to the transcendental method",[46] which was made famous by Kant in his *Critique of Pure Reason*, influencing the whole of post-Kantian philosophy, and has been practiced by the Transcendental Thomists. This method consists in turning my attention from the object to my cognition of it.

In the second step of my argument for God's existence, I turned from direct intellection of a scientific fact to know the *esse* of that intellection. Because of these two procedures – direct cognition of a scientific fact and introspecting the *esse* of that cognition – I think that the title of this essay is justified. Has not this inquiry established that my own direct human thinking is a sign of the existence of God?

9

A FACT OF KNOWLEDGE

A FACT OF KNOWLEDGE
AND GOD'S EXISTENCE

B esides the traditional Five Ways of proving that God exists, there is another way, the dynamism of the human intellect. Those unimpressed by the Five Ways may find this other way more acceptable. It is in this context that I have written the following essay on the mind's dynamism.

In this study, I intend to clarify the ultimate goal of human intellectual activity by a triple process.[1] First, I shall propose a question. Second, I shall explain the meaning of the terms used in the question. Third, I shall present the procedure used to answer the question.

First, here is the principal question of this treatise: Knowing what intelligible object completely satisfies my mind's natural appetite which, on the one hand, affirms that a tree covered with white blossoms exists (a fact of experience) and, on the other hand, simultaneously transcends knowing that this apple tree *is*?

Second, the terms employed in formulating the above question will be explained as follows: mind as natural appetite, affirming activity, formal object of the mind's natural appetite, affirmed object as transcended, affirmed object as limited.

Third, my procedure in this discourse will be to use a disjunctive syllogism and two hypothetical syllogisms in order to establish that knowing the proposition, "Pure *Esse* is," is true, answers the above question.

My Mind as Natural Appetite

Mental natural appetite is the possible intellect actuated by an intelligible species. In order to understand the above sentence, I shall explain the meaning of the following terms: natural appetite, possible intellect, intelligible species.

Why I call my mind a natural appetite can be understood easily from the following example. If I am aware that I judge a tree *is*, if I then affirm that this blue jay on the lawn exists and subsequently acknowledge the existence of a certain student in my office, I am conscious of movement in my mental activities. Consciousness of this intellectual motion leads me to conclude that this change has a source, which I name my mental natural appetite. Whenever a student questions a teacher, the very asking of the question shows the student's mental appetite to know. In Aquinas' words, a human being's "intellect by nature desires to know."[2]

A true story illustrates this mental natural appetite. Several years ago, a college graduate who had received a fellowship from a prestigious university to do graduate work in a highly specialized field wrote to me, "I am not going to attend graduate school because, after eight weeks spent in Europe, I want to know more about art, history, literature, music, and philosophy." This statement describes the graduate's insatiable curiosity, her intellect's natural tendency to know.

That I designate my mind a "possible" intellect may be disclosed from the following fact that anyone can experience internally. I can change from intellectually grasping the meaning of a tree to apprehending what a bird or what a person is. Because of this ability to move from thinking about one meaning to apprehending another meaning, I name my intellect "possible."

Directing my possible intellect to focus on the meaning of a tree, instead of grasping the meaning of an animal, is the precise role of the intelligible species, actuating my possible intellect. How the intelligible species determines my possible intellect requires a brief reflection on mental knowing.

An example will assist in elucidating the meaning of mental knowing. When I eat an apple, my hand picks up the apple, puts it in my mouth; and then I consume the apple. In this process, I am united with the apple; in a sense, I am the apple; and the apple is changed. I call this union a physical union.

On the other hand, at the moment I know that a tree covered with blossoms *exists*, this knowing has no need to get outside itself to attain the tree known. In this activity, I am united with the tree; in other words, I am the tree; and the tree is not changed. I call this union an intentional union.

How can I be the tree if I can't put the tree in my mind like I put the apple in my mouth when I eat it? This question is answered on two levels: the sense level and the intellectual level.

On the *sense* level, in order to see the white aspect of a tree, my power of sight must receive from the white item a likeness of the white object. I call this likeness a sensible species. With this sensible likeness of white actuating my power of sight, I can by that sense power proceed to see the white color of the tree. And so, the sensible species actuates my power of sight in order that, with my power of sight, I see the color of an object.

On the *intellectual* level, in order to apprehend tree, my intellectual power, in some way, must receive from the tree a likeness of tree. I call this likeness an intelligible species.

The process of receiving this intelligible species is more complicated than receiving a sensible species from the sensed object. The reason is that apprehending trees involves knowing the meaning of "tree" in general. This is evident because in saying the word "tree," I signify that I know the meaning of "tree" in general. How can this particular apple tree covered with white blossoms produce an intelligible likeness of treeness in general so that I then grasp the meaning of tree in general? In other words, how can a particular tree cause, in my intellect, a likeness of "tree" in general?

Aquinas answers that the image of a white covered item conjured up in my *imagination* cannot produce the likeness of tree in general in my *intellect*.[3] Therefore, my soul, in addition to my intellect, has another power, called the agent intellect, whose sole purpose is to remove particularity from the particular images, like the representation of the white colored tree, so that there results in my intellect a likeness of meaning in general, as the likeness of tree in general, an intelligible species. Consequently, the intelligible species must actuate my possible intellect in order that, with my mind, I apprehend the meaning of a particular object.

To summarize, my possible intellect informed by an intelligible species is a natural appetite desiring not just an act of understanding, not solely an existent, but instead an act of understanding an existent. To state this another way, the intellect is a power specified by an operation which, in turn, is specified by the object.

Affirming Activity

Having completed my analysis of my possible intellect as a natural appetite, I now examine the affirming activity proceeding from that natural appetite by asking three questions. What kind of judgment occurs when I affirm that a blossom-laden tree exists? What is the reality of the activity itself of judging that this tree with green leaves exists? What type of knowing process do I employ in coming to affirm the reality of this judging activity?

What kind of judgment occurs when I affirm that a blossom-laden tree exists? Such an act of affirming is direct judging, i.e., knowing an object some of whose characteristics are sensible. The white and green colors of the tree are sensible since I know them by the power of sight. The *existence* component of the tree is not sensible but intelligible. The reason is that, through my power of sight, I do not know that radio waves exist in this room.

But I do know these waves exist. Therefore, with another power, my possible intellect, I know both that radio waves exist and that the tree is. Hence, affirming that the blossom-covered tree exists is direct judging.

But what is the reality of directly judging that this flower laden tree exists? The act of affirming, "A tree exists," is an intentional *esse*. By this I mean that when I know the tree *is*, I am the tree – without destroying it – by an *esse* other than the substantial *esse* by which I have existed all my life. In other words, intentional *esse* means that to know is to be the other as *other* (the other is not changed), not by substantial *esse*. Thus, a philosophical analysis has divulged that the act of affirming, "A tree exists," is an intentional *esse*.

Due to the ambiguity of the English word "is," in this essay, I have used the Latin infinitive *esse* to indicate clearly that I imply either the substantial act of existing, as expressed in the proposition, "This tree *is*," or cognitional existence as expressed in the proposition, "To know is to be the object." On the other hand, "is" may designate a logical predicate, as in the proposition: a triangle is...

With which knowing process do I know the intentional *esse* of directly judging that a tree *is*? To know the above *esse*, I deliberately turn from direct cognition to knowing through philosophical analysis the intentional *esse* of that cognition. I call this act of internal witnessing introspection.

FORMAL OBJECT OF THE DESIRE

Having scrutinized my mental natural appetite and my affirming activity, I now raise the question, What is the total formal object of my mind? By "total formal object of my mind" I signify the aspect, the common denominator, present in every object knowable by my intellect. So far, in this study, I have been conscious of two objects attained by my mind, the existence of a blossom covered tree (known by direct judging) and the intentional *esse* of that direct judging (known through philosophical analysis by intro-spection). On a wider scale, existence belongs to all sensible items in the universe and to all not sensible items, like radio waves and acts of intellection. The aspect common to both the existence of sensible items and to the existence of not sensible items is intelligible existence, i.e., existence able to be known by my mind. Therefore, the total formal object of my mental natural appetite is intelligible existence.

Let me illustrate this point with respect to the power of sight. It is readily granted that color reflecting light must be present in every visible object and is therefore the total formal object of the power of sight. If an item is colorless or perfectly transparent, I do not see it. Clearly, existence, either in a sensible item or in a not sensible item, must be present in every intelligible object. Accordingly, just as color reflecting light is the total formal object of my *sight*, so intelligible existence is the total formal object of my *intellect*.

AFFIRMED OBJECT AS TRANSCENDED

Moreover, in its act of affirming, "A certain tree exists," my mind transcends, goes beyond, my knowing that this tree *is*. This transcending dynamism is revealed by the same example I used to establish my mind as a natural appetite. If I notice that I affirm a tree exists, then judge this blue jay is, and subsequently acknowledge that a certain student exists, I am conscious that my mind, at the same time that it affirmed a tree exists, also went beyond knowing that existent towards knowing other objects. Whenever anyone questions an item, the very asking of the question manifests that the questioner's mind transcends knowing that item. This transcending dynamism of the human mind's natural appetite is an undeniable fact that anyone can experience internally.

But this rebounding knowing activity originates not

from affirming a tree's existence but rather from my rest-less mental natural appetite judging that a tree exists. Thus my mind's many knowing activities bring to light not only that my mind is a natural appetite but also that it simulta-neously transcends, surges beyond, these same affir-mations.

AFFIRMED OBJECT AS LIMITED

I directly experience the tree as limited because the above successive affirmations exhibit that affirming a tree exists does not completely satisfy my mental natural appetite, and hence is limited. If affirming a tree exists did completely satisfy my mind, I would not have gone on to affirm that other objects exist.

An example from the world of art illustrates the point here. A visitor to Madrid's Prado Museum successively views El Greco's *St. John the Evangelist*, and the same artist's *Christ Carrying the Cross*. If asked, the visitor would cer-tainly admit that, since the first painting did not satisfy completely the visitor's aesthetic taste for beauty, the mas-terpiece had limited aesthetic beauty. Similarly, the fact that affirming a tree exists does not completely satisfy the im-pulse of the mind, manifests the limitation of the tree.

SOLUTION: FIRST STAGE

At this point, the meaning of the question – Knowing what intelligible object does completely satisfy my mind's natural appetite which, on the one hand, affirms that a tree exists and, on the other hand, simultaneously transcends knowing that this tree exists – should be clear. I now proceed to the first stage of the answer, a disjunctive syllogism.

The above mental natural appetite is completely sat-isfied by either knowing non-being, or affirming "Another finite being *is*," or by cognition of the totality of finite be-ings, or by knowing that Pure *Esse is*.

The first three members of this disjunctive proposi-tion are unsatisfactory. Clearly, knowing non-being does not satisfy my mind since the intellect's total formal object is intelligible existence, not non-being. Also affirming that another finite being *is* does not completely satiate my mind. As was previously explained, a limited being, by definition, is a being not fully satisfying my mind. Finally, knowing the totality of finite beings does not entirely appease my mind. For this totality is a totality of beings not fully satisfying my intellect.

Therefore, granting that what fully satisfies my mind's transcending desire is intelligible and granting that the above disjunctive proposition lists all possible alternatives, it follows that my mind's transcending dynamism is completely fulfilled by knowing that Pure *Esse*, the Infinite Being, *is*.

SOLUTION: SECOND STAGE

Since Sartre and Camus claim that the teleological drive of my mind is in vain, I must establish that knowing there is an Infinite Being means not just affirming a *concept* but knowing there is an actually *existing* Infinite. I shall do this by formulating two hypothetical syllogisms.

First, Infinite Being is internally possible, or contains compatible perfections. For if Infinite Existence is intrinsically *im*possible, any degree of existence, like intentional *esse*, is intrinsically *im*possible. But it is false that intentional *esse* is intrinsically impossible since I have already introspected, through philosophical analysis, the intentional *esse* of my direct cognition about a material being. Therefore, it is false that Infinite Existence is intrinsically impossible.

Repeating the classic example of a hypothetical syllogism illustrates the force of the reasoning process in this type of syllogism: If it rains, the roof is wet; if it is false that the roof is wet, it is false that it is raining.

Second, Infinite Being is externally possible, or is a being whose causes for existence are present. For example, electric lights would be extrinsically possible on a pleasure boat equipped with a battery. Infinite Being is externally possible since such a Being is its own sufficient reason for existing and hence is independent of causes. If Infinite Existence depends on a cause for existence, the Infinite would lack a perfection found in its cause, originator of existence. Now it is false that Infinite Being lacks a perfection because such a being would be finite and would not completely satisfy my mind's impulse. But through my disjunctive syllogism, I have previously established that only *knowing there is an Infinite Being* fully satisfies my mind's transcending dynamism. Therefore, it is false that Infinite Existence depends on a cause for its existence.

With the internal and external possibility of Infinite Being established, I can now assert that what completely satisfies my mind is knowing that there is an actually existing Infinite Being.[4]

An Objection

Even though the previous disjunctive and hypothetical syllogisms have established that I know there is an actually existing Infinite Being, these syllogisms have not made this Infinite Being physically present to me.

My answer is as follows. *Esse* has two meanings. First, it means the act of existing as expressed in the statement: this colorful tree exists. Second, *esse* signifies a logical predicate which posits the subject with all its predicates as in the logical proposition: triangle *is*.... The conclusion of my disjunctive and hypothetical syllogisms signifies not that I know the *esse* of God, but that I know the logical proposition – "There is an actually existing Infinite" – is true from the effect of God, namely, the transcending dynamism of my mind.

An example explains this reply. If I release a pencil three feet above the desk, the pencil falls to the desk. I see the falling pencil. I know gravity attracted the released pencil to the desk. I do not see gravity but I know the logical proposition, "There is gravity," is true from the effect of the falling pencil. In a similar manner, I am conscious of my mind's transcending motion roving from affirming "One material thing *is*" to affirming "Another material thing *is*."

Also I know that understanding there is an actually existing infinite attracts my mental transcending desire. But I am not conscious of Pure *Esse*; however, I do know the logical proposition, "There is an actually existing Infinite Being," is true from the effect of God, the transcending impulse of my mind.

To summarize, just as gravity is continually attracting the pencil, so knowing there is an actually existing infinite is constantly attracting my mind's transcending desire moving from affirming, "One material thing *is*," to affirming, "Another material thing *is*."

CONCLUSION

Through the solution to the question of this essay, I do not know God, "the reality that encompasses everything," as one particular being alongside other particular beings, or as one particular being above the world – otherwise God would be another finite being.[5] But I only know that there is an actually existing infinite term of my intellect's dynamism.[6] Wherefore, an analysis of my mind's dynamism is another way of proving that God exists.

The language of poetry may be accommodated to describe my mind's transcending motion towards the Infinite.

> "A man's reach must exceed his grasp.
> Or what's a heaven for."[7]

10 NATURAL THEOLOGY

NATURAL THEOLOGY AND RELIGIOUS VALUE

D oes a believer reading natural theology find religious value in that study? In *Introduction to Existentialism*, Marjorie Grene wrote that "proofs" of God's Existence are not necessary for a believer.[1] Is this correct? Since an answer is understandable only in the light of the question, I shall clarify the question by defining its three terms: believer, natural theology, and religious value.[2]

In this essay, the term *believer* signifies a Christian who has faith in the facts revealed by the words of God. Here a believer is not someone who believes in a theology. In my view, a believer is a person having faith in a reality as it is known from the Bible and Tradition.[3]

Natural theology, on the other hand, is the science by which, from a knowledge of sensible beings, I demonstrate both the Existence of God and the Attributes of God. These demonstrations, acts of the intellect, are both horizontal and vertical. They are horizontal because they always begin with my knowledge of sensible beings. They are also vertical since, through analysis of this latter knowledge, in opposition to Kant's view, I vault to the affirmation of the truth of various propositions about God's Existence, Goodness,

Omnipresence, and so forth, from the effects of God. The paradigm of natural theology for this study is Thomas Aquinas's philosophy according to which the First Cause, the Subsisting Act of Existing, conserves the existence of all limited beings, concurs with every action of finite beings, creates all contingent beings, and attracts the intellect and will of every human being.[4]

Finally, *religious value*, as employed in this treatise, encompasses any item which can foster those activities by which a believer talks to God. This description of religious value has two components. The first component is the item itself, which encourages religious actions. The second component includes these same acts by which a person of faith, in turn, speaks to God.

Here are two examples of the first component. First, the starry heavens were items promoting religious activities for Ignatius Loyola, but not for some astronomer interested only in calculating the distance between the Earth and Mars. For the contemplation of the stars stirred Ignatius to thank God, the source of the grandeur and the beauty of the heavens. A second example of an item inspiring religious response centers around the scripture text, "What does it profit a man to gain the whole world and suffer the loss of his own soul."[5] This text would not qualify as a religious item for a student concerned merely with comparing the above passage with an ancient manuscript. But the quotation was such an item for Francis Xavier, since it moved him to dedicate his life to the service of God. In these examples, the starry heavens and a scripture text qualify as first components of religious value, namely, items that stimulated actions by which two believers conversed with God.

The second component of religious value, activities by which a believer communicates with God, needs further elaboration. These actions include acts of praise, giving thanks, asking for forgiveness, requesting favors, submitting to God's Will, and even talking with God as with a friend. A religious person may express complete dependence on the Deity or make a total dedication to God to the extent of adopting a very austere way of life.[6] Accordingly, these actions include acts of the intellect and acts of the will. Putting the above two components together, I maintain that religious value belongs to any item, such as a natural event or a text, that can cause acts like praise or giving thanks by which a believer speaks to God.

By now the question, Does a believer reading natural theology find religious value in that discipline, should be easy to understand. I don't ask whether reading a natural theology text, perusing how a knowledge of sensible beings leads to knowledge about a First Cause, actually will prompt every believer to thank God. But I do inquire whether studying such a natural theology passage can incline a believer to praise God, i.e., has religious value. In short, my question is, Can talking about God in a natural theology class help a believer talk to God in prayer?

Blaise Pascal and William James

Before presenting Joseph DeFinance's view that reading natural theology can attract religious acts in a believer – in other words, does have religious value – I shall describe briefly the positions of two philosophers, Blaise Pascal and William James, who deny that studying natural theology has religious consequence. By this procedure, DeFinance's position "when put on the defensive [...] comes to be examined with more thoroughness, grasped with more clarity and proclaimed with more emphasis."[7] Thus can doubt, raised by adversaries, end in certitude.

In his *Mémorial*, found after his death, sewn into his coat, Blaise Pascal stated that God is "the God of Abraham, God of Isaac, God of Jacob, not of the philosophers and savants."[8] And so, the God of philosophy is not the God which a believer worships. Therefore, for Pascal, the rational investigation of God is irrelevant for religious conscience.

Confining my examination of William James's position on the subject under consideration to his beautiful classic, *Varieties of Religious Experience*, I find that, by applying the touchstone of his pragmatic criterion of truth to God's Existence and God's Metaphysical Attributes, he assigned religious value to the former but not to the latter. In the above book, the author described the pragmatic criterion of truth as "that which works well on the whole."[9]

James held that God's Existence fulfilled this criterion because it "actually exerts an influence, raises our center of personal energy, and produces regenerative effects unattainable in other ways."[10] In other words, God's Existence is known only through religious experience.

On the other hand, he asserted that God's Metaphysical Attributes failed to meet his pragmatic criterion since they had no religious consequence for him. For example, he asked, "What specific act can I perform in order to adapt myself better to God's Simplicity?"[11] Consequently, according to his *Varieties of Religious Experience*, I can understand why James ascribed religious value to God's Existence but not to God's Metaphysical Attributes.

DeFinance: God's Existence

In contrast to Pascal and James, Joseph DeFinance in *Theologia Naturalis* explained that both Thomas Aquinas' demonstration of God's Existence and his arguments for the Divine Attributes have religious value for a believer. Following the order in his book, I take up the proof for God's Existence before discussing the Attributes of God.

With the two topics to be examined before me, I now introduce a note of caution. This question can be answered fully only by theology because the queen of the sciences takes up the profound problem of the connection between the human intellect and faith. Here the subject is discussed as far as the scope of philosophy allows.[12]

DeFinance granted that subjective certitude about God's Existence, i.e., certitude based on internal religious experience, does help a believer talk to God for two reasons. First, through experience of illumination or inspiration, a believer may develop a personal relationship with God. Secondly, this religious activity attains God as *real*

because conversation with God is possible only for someone who believes that God truly exists.[13]

But DeFinance's main point is that Aquinas's rational inquiry concerning God's Existence is of great importance for a believer's acts of prayer and adoration, because
such an investigation provides a believer with objective
certitude about God's extramental Existence. Aquinas'
proof about God's Existence achieves this objective certitude since the argument, using the light of reason alone,
begins with the affirmation that a sensible being exists and
it ends by inferring that there is an extramental First Cause
to the extent that a denial of God's Existence results in a
contradiction in the sensible being itself. All this follows
for the reason that, in Aquinas' view, the existence of a sensible being necessarily depends on the continual influence
of the First Cause, just like daylight depends on the sun.
Thus the certitude is based both horizontally (on knowing
that an extramental sensible being exists) and vertically (on
affirming that the proposition, "There is an extramental First
Cause," is true).

Objective certitude about God's Existence attained
through natural theology is of great importance to a
believer's internal adherence to God for three reasons. First,
a believer in possession of this kind of certitude knows that
acts of prayer and adoration are not empty and illusory.
Secondly, such a believer can long continue having certitude about God's Existence; for natural theology provides
a believer with responses to contemporary objections raised
by adversaries. Thirdly, equipped with natural theology, a
believer as a whole, not only through religious experience
but also by rational cognition, adheres to God.[14] In summary, objective certitude about God's Existence can assist
a believer by bringing peace to the mind and stability and
purpose to life.

Recently two students remarked to me about demonstrations of God's Existence having religious value. One
student said, "I never felt closer to God than during my
study of the proofs for God's Existence." The other student
observed, "When I understood the Fourth Way, I had a spiri-

tual experience. I realized for the first time the unity of all things because God is in all things."

Here is another example of how philosophical knowledge of God's Existence can have religious value. I know from the argument for God's Existence that I exist because God desires me into being and keeps me in being. God is, as it would seem, not a task master, not a tyrant, but madly in love with me, is always attracted to me. If in response to God's love for me, I develop an intimate relationship of friendship and love with God, the study of the proofs for God's Existence will have religious value for me.

DeFinance: God's Attributes

Having described DeFinance's view that demonstrating God's Existence can determine a believer to praise God, does have religious value, I shall now consider the same author's position that the Attributes of God known through natural theology also have religious value. My task will consist in naming the precise religious acts that correlate with the various Divine Attributes.

Divine Infinity is the basis for the reverence with which a believer should approach God in prayer and worship. For it is through Infinity that God presents Himself to a believer as a being of tremendous majesty, a light shining too brightly for the believer. Whereas before this Infinity, a finite being perceives itself as dust and ashes. To this irremovable difference between God and a human person a believer can respond appropriately only by an attitude of reverence in all religious acts.[15]

Even the analogy of being, the warp and woof of Aquinas' natural theology, has religious value. According to this analogy, being can be said of God and of finite being, both in a similar sense and in a completely different sense. The *similarity* between God and finite being satisfies the religious person's desire for some cognition of God, while the *difference* between God and limited being corresponds to the believer's attitude of, at times, praising God by silence.[16]

Divine Simplicity, Unicity, and Omnipresence can evoke religious acts in a believer. Divine Simplicity is an ideal towards which a religious person advances by striving to perform all human acts for the love of God. God's Unicity is the object of that charity by which a believer fulfills the first of the Ten Commandments. Divine Omnipresence greatly facilitates the religious soul seeking to do God's Will in all the events of life.[17]

The doctrine that God knows all things other than Himself greatly consoles a religious person for two reasons. First, prayer has no meaning unless God knows me. Secondly, God judges not according to appearances but according to truth.[18]

Divine Liberty is also necessary for prayer to have its full meaning. The reason is that if God does not will and love others freely, prayer would be like a magic formula.[19]

Divine Creation and Divine Concurrence are fundamental for a religious person trying to develop the key virtue of humility. According to the former Attribute, God freely gives all creatures their total reality; according to the latter, all creatures truly act, yet in their total activity they depend on God.[20] This total dependence on God obviously grounds St. Augustine's definition of humility, "the complete consciousness of our entire dependence on God."[21]

Finally, Providence, that God cares for me, and Omnipotence, that nothing is impossible with God, justify peace and trust, requisites for a religious person wanting to adhere to God.[22]

CONCLUSION

To complete my presentation of natural theology's religious value, I return to the objections proposed at the beginning of this discourse.

To Marjorie Grene, I reply that "proofs" of God's Existence are necessary for a believer who wants to answer the difficulties proposed by adversaries. To Blaise Pascal, I suggest that the God of philosophy and the God of religion are not opposed. For the God whose Existence natural theology demonstrates has the same Attributes — Infinity, Omnipresence, Omnipotence, etc. — that a religious person attributes to God. However, I admit that the mode of attaining God differs for a philosopher and for a religious person. The philosopher talks *about* God; the religious person talks *to* God.[23] To William James, I respond that Divine Simplicity, a Metaphysical Attribute of God, has religious value as I designated above.

To my initial question, I am now in a position to answer with the conclusion that reading a natural theology text can have religious value for a believer, that talking about God in a philosophy class can help a believer talk to God in prayer. So, there can be a bridge between the God of philosophy and the God of religion.

Natural theology's religious value has two advantages. First, it may provide a reply to a college student's question, "Why should I study metaphysics?" The answer is that natural theology with religious value for a believer is the heart of metaphysics. Secondly, it may highlight Aldous Huxley's suggestion in *Perennial Philosophy* that the solution to the basic problem of contemporary society is for every human being to acknowledge dependence on a Supreme Being.[24] That I depend on God is a truth established by natural theology. Should this truth influence a believer to acknowledge dependence on God, such a truth would have religious value for that person.

And this is the point of my meditation, that reading natural theology can have religious value for a believer. However, with the machine age obscuring the metaphysical order, is it any wonder that, today, people so easily forget their necessary dependence on a Supreme Being?

To summarize this book, I have found in the Universe the following finger prints of God: a good with a beginning and an end (Anselm), *esse* of a finite being, motion, different degrees of existing, intentional *esse* of direct cognition, the dynamism of the human mind (Aquinas).

In short, inferring God's Existence is demonstrating God's Existence by showing that a denial of the logical proposition, "God is," is contradictory.

NOTES

A complimentary copy of STUDENT MANUAL (with diagrams and 56 review questions) for this book may be obtained by writing to J. Brady, S.J., 5133 Forest, Kansas City, MO 64110.

PROLOGUE

1. M. Holloway, *An Introduction to Natural Theology* (New York, 1959), p. 48.
   M. Adler, *How to Think about God* (New York, 1980), p. 108.

CHAPTER SEVEN

1. H. Bouillard, *The Knowledge of God*, transl. S.D. Femiano (New York, 1968), p. 65.

2. *Ibid.*, p. 75.

3. M. Holloway, *An Introduction to Natural Theology* (New York, 1959), p. 45.

4. St. Anselm, *St. Anselm's Proslogion*, transl. M.J. Charlesworth (London, 1979), p. 161.

5. H. Bouillard, *op. cit.*, p. 85.

6. *Ibid.*

7. J. Pieper, *Scholasticism*, transl. Richard and Clara Winston (New York, 1964), p. 66.

8. T. Horvath, "Presenting this Issue", in *Ultimate Reality and Meaning*, Vol. 14, no. 2, p. 83.

9. St. Thomas Aquinas, *Summa Theol.*, transl. T. Gilby (Garden City, 1969) I, 2, 1, rep. to obj. 2.

10. Immanuel Kant, *Critique of Pure Reason*, transl. N. Smith (New York, 1929). pp. 504, 502, 504.

11. Aquinas, *op. cit.*, I, 2, 1, c.

CHAPTER EIGHT

1. H. Klocker, *The God Within* (Washington, 1982), p. ix.

2. T. Aquinas, *On Being and Essence*, ch. 5.

3. I. Kant, *Critique of Pure Reason*, transl. N. Smith (New York, 1933), pp. 507-514.

4. J. Maritain, *The Degrees of Knowledge*, transl. G.B. Phelan (New York, 1959), p. 65.

5. G. Smith argues in this way, *Natural Theology* (New York, 1966), p. 38.

6. H. Renard, *Philosophy of Being* (Milwaukee, 1957), p. 167.

7. J. Maritain, *Approaches to God*, transl. P. O'Reilly (New York, 1954), p. 35.

8. I. Kant, *Prolegomena to Any Future Metaphysics*, transl. L. Beck (New York, 1950), p. 49.

9. D. Hume, *A Treatise of Human Nature* (Baltimore, 1969), p. 300.

10. *Critique of Pure Reason*, op. cit., p. 508.

11. *Ibid.*, p. 510.

12. *Ibid.*, p. 502.

13. *Ibid.*, p. 506

14. *The Degrees of Knowledge*, op. cit., p. 80.

CHAPTER NINE

1. S. Thomas Aquinas, *De Veritate*, X, art. 12, reply.

2. G. Smith, *Natural Theology* (New York, 1966), pp. 107-113.

3. E. Sillem, *Ways of Thinking about God* (New York, 1960), pp. 1-183.

4. *Ibid.*, p. 77.

CHAPTER TEN

1. This manner of expressing a judgment of similarity between existents is taken from J. O'Brien, "Analogy and the Fourth Way," in *Wisdom in Depth*, ed. V. Daues (Milwaukee, 1965), p. 177.

2. Aristotle, *Meta.*, VII, 8, 1034a 5-8.

3. For more complete explanations of a real relation of quantity cf. G. Klubertanze, *Introduction to the Philosophy of Being*, 2nd ed. (New York, 1963), pp. 272-273, and L. Sweeney, *A Metaphysics of Authentic Existentialism* (Englewood Cliffs, 1965), pp. 190-201.

4. S. Thomas Aquinas, *Summa Theol.*, transl. J. Brady, S.J., I, 2, 3c.

5. *Capita quaedam praelectionum Theologiae Naturalis* (Romae, 1963-1964), pp. 319-363.

6. *Ibid.*, p. 337.

7. *Ibid.*, p. 361.

8. *Ibid.*, p. 338.

9. *Ibid.*, p. 338, 361.

10. Cf. E. Gilson, *The Christian Philosophy of St. Thomas Aquinas*, transl. L. Shook (New York, 1956), p. 44. Aquinas' "metaphysics of being as being 'consignifies' existence. It does not 'signify' it unless precisely it uses the second operation of the understanding and employs all the resources of the judgment."

11. Cf. S. Thomas Aquinas, *De Ver.*, transl. R. Schmidt (Chicago, 1954), XXII, 2ad 2. "All cognitive beings also know God implicitly in any object of knowledge. Just as nothing has the note of appetibility except by a likeness to the first goodness, so nothing is knowable except by a likeness to the first truth."

12. This line of reasoning is developed fully below, Chap. Twelve.

13. Cf. J. Collins, *God in Modern Philosophy* (Chicago, 1959), p. 399, and J. Maritain, *Approaches to God* (New York, 1954), p. 13.

14. Cf. G. Smith, *Natural Theology* (New York, 1966), p. 35.

15. Cf. A. Korinek, *op. cit.*, pp. 338, 359, 360.

16. S. Thomas Aquinas, *Summa Theol.*, transl. J. Brady, S.J. *op. cit.*, I, 2, 3c.

17. "Les Cinq Voies de Saint Thomas," in *L'Existence de Dieu*, 2nd ed. (Tournai, 1963), pp. 211-212.

18. S. Thomas Aquinas, *Summa Theol.*, transl. J. Anderson, *op. cit.*, I, 4, 3c.

19. Cf. A. Korinek, *Problema Creationis et Providentiae* (Romae, 1964), p. 56.

126   New Approaches to God

20. A. Boekraad, *Philosophy of God* (Loyola University, 1965), p. 57.

21. F. Wilhelmsen, "The Christian Understanding of Being: A Thomistic Reading," in *The Intercollegiate Review*, Winter-Spring (1978), p. 93.

22. S. Thomas Aquinas, *De Pot.*, transl. L. Shapcote (Westminister, 1965), III, 1 ad 17.

23. M. Holloway, *An Introduction to Natural Theology* (New York, 1959), p. 127.

24. L. Charlier, *op. cit.*, p. 210.

25. F. Genuyt, *The Mystery of God*, transl. J. Pilch (New York, 1968), p. 44.

26. A. Huxley, *The Perennial Philosophy* (New York, 1962), p. 172.

27. J. Maritain, *Integral Humanism*, transl. J. Evans (New York, 1968), p. 207.

CHAPTER ELEVEN

1. For an approach to God's existence with a similar starting point cf. Jean-Dominique Robert, O.P., *Approche Contemporaine d'une Affirmation de Dieu* (Bruges, 1962), pp. 9-221.

2. Two author assert that Kant considered only the content of knowing, not the activity itself of human knowing. E. Coreth, S.J., *Metaphysics*, transl. J. Donceel, S.J. (New York, 1968), p. 52. J. Donceel, S.J., "A Case in Reason for God's Existence," in *God Knowable and Unknowable*, ed. R.J. Roth, S.J. (New York, 1973), p. 174.

3. Notice the following description of experience in J. Marechal, S.J., "Au Seuil de la Metaphysique: Abstraction ou Intuition," in *Melanges Joseph Marechal*, Tome I, *Oeuvres* (Paris, 1950), p. 117. "We place ourselves now outside of metaphysics, at the heart of that immediate and concrete knowledge which our external and internal senses acquire and which we generally call experience." Transl. J.M.B.

4. This example is taken from St. Augustine, *On the Gospel of John*, in *A Select Library of the Nicene and Post - Nicene Fathers*, vol. 7, ed. P. Schaff (New York, 1887-1892), p. 335.

5. *Dialogue with Myself* (New York, 1966), p. 86.

6. *The Openness of Being* (Philadelphia, 1971), p. 86.

7. This negative analysis is from J. Maritain, *The Degrees of Knowledge*, transl. G.B. Phelan (New York, 1959), pp. 111-115.

8. This positive analysis is adapted from J. Maritain, *ibid.*

9. "Better" more appropriately describes the perfection of existing here than "bigger." Cf. above, Chap. Ten.

10. A study of pertinent texts in Aquinas reveals that for the Angelic Doctor cog-

nition is the existence of the thing known in the knower, according to an article by J. Owens, C.S.S.R., "Cognition as Existence," in the *Proceedings of the American Catholic Philosophical Association*, XLVIII (1974), 75.

11. This example is given by I. Kant, *Prolegomena to Any Future Metaphysics*, ed. L. Beck (Indianapolis, 1950), p. 49.

12. Compare this definition with the following definition of perception given by E. Mascall, *op. cit.*, p. 99. Perception is the direct, mediated activity in which the intellect in and through the sensible particular grasps the intelligible, extra-mental being. Likewise compare my definition of direct knowledge with the following description of direct cognition stated by V.J. Bourke in his article "Invalid Proofs for God's Existence," in the *Proceedings of the American Catholic Philosophical Association*, XXVIII (1954), 37. Using both sense powers and intellect we first directly grasp bodily things existing extra-mentally.

13. Cf. Mascall, *op. cit.*, p. 46.

14. In his *Method in Theology* (New York, 1972) p. 8, B. Lonergan, S.J., cautions that introspection is not an inward ocular glance.

15. Cf. Mascall, *op. cit.*, p. 46.

16. Coreth calls this the turn to the transcendental method in which I turn my attention from the object to my cognition of it. *Op. cit.*, p. 23.

17. Cf. J. Marechal, S.J., *A Marechal Reader*, transl. and ed. J. Donceel, S.J. (New York, 1970), p. 203. Sensibility, an intrinsically material knowing power, is not a self-transparent faculty.

18. For other types of intellectual activity cf. Lonergan, *op. cit.*, p. 15.

19. Robert, *op. cit.*, pp. 204-205, proposes the question of his study as follows. How does one ultimately harmonize these paradoxical aspects revealed in scientific truth: a contingently existing act of human thought considering necessary intelligibilities creates one scientific truth which is in many minds?

20. Man has an unquenchable thirst for knowledge according to J. De Finance, S.J., *Essai sur L'Agir Humain* (Rome, 1962), p. 125.

21. *Rep.*, X, 596a.

22. I. Kant, *Critique of Pure Reason*, transl. N. Smith (New York, 1933), p. 504.

23. *Ibid.*

24. *Prolegomena to Any Future Metaphysics, op. cit.*, p. 49.

25. *Critique of Pure Reason, op. cit.*, pp. 504, 502.

26. *Ibid.*, p. 506

27. *Ibid.*, p. 143.

28. *Ibid.*, p. 82.

29. *Ibid.*, p. 505.

30. Cf. Maritain, *op. cit.*, p. 58

31. Cf. Robert, *op. cit.*, p. 155.

32. Cf. *Maritain, op. cit.*, p. 57.

33. Cf. Robert, *op. cit.*, pp. 139-140.

34. "Naturalism Reconsidered," in *Contemporary Philosophic Problems*, ed. Y. Krikorian and A. Edel (New York 1959), pp. 337-349.

35. *Ibid.*, p. 344.

36. *Ibid.*, p. 340.

37. *Ibid.*

38. This view is proposed by N. Clarke, S.J., "Analytic Philosophy and Language about God," in *Christian Philosophy and Religious Renewal*, ed. G. McLean, O.M.I. (Washington, 1967), pp. 48 F.

39. Cf. Maritain, *op. cit.*, p. 113.

40. Experiencing is the same as being conscious according to Lonergan, *op. cit.*, pp. 6-20. In this view sensory experiencing and mental experiencing would be the same as being sensorially conscious and being mentally conscious respectively.

41. Cf. Coreth, *op. cit.*, p. 29. Infinite Being is never revealed to us as an object, but it is known by us only in the finite beings whose ground it is.

42. Cf. Owens, *op. cit.*, p. 81.

43. Cf. Robert, *op. cit.*, p. 186.

44. *Leisure the Basis of Culture*, transl. A. Dru (New York, 1963), p. 106.

45. *Psalm* 139; transl. The Liturgical Press (Collegeville, 1961).

46. Coreth, *op. cit.*, p. 23.

47. Transcendental method functions similarly in the *Critique of Pure Reason* and in our essay because both demand a turning from the object. But there is a difference. Kant turns to examine the way we know objects. *Op. cit.*, p. 59. In this study we turn to affirm the intentional *esse* of direct intellection.

CHAPTER TWELVE

1. For an approach to God with a similar starting point cf. the following books: J.

DeFevre, S.J., *La Preuve Réelle de Dieu* (Paris, 1953), pp. 7-144, J. Donceel, S.J., *The Searching Mind* (Notre Dame, 1979), pp. 55-92, J. Javaux, *Une Affirmation Raisonnée de Dieu* (Paris, 1974), pp. 5-128, and K. Rahner, S.J.,*Foundations of Christian Faith*, transl. W.V. Dych (New York, 1978), pp. 44-89.

2. Cf. S. Thomas Aquinas, *The Soul*, transl. John Patrick Rowan (St. Louis, 1949), p. 172.

3. *Ibid.*, p. 51.

4. This exposition is adapted from Javaux, *op. cit.*, pp. 94-98.

5. W. Kasper, *The God of Jesus Christ*, transl. M.J. O'Connell (New York, 1984), p. 26.

6. Cf. Rahner, *op. cit.*, p. 64.

7. R. Browning, "Andrea del Sarto," in *Victorian and Later English Poets*, E. J. Stephens et.al. (New York, 1937), p. 338.

CHAPTER THIRTEEN

1. M. Grene, *Introduction to Existentialism* (Chicago, 1959), p. 132.

2. W. Kasper, *The God of Jesus Christ*, transl. Matthew J. O'Connell (New York, 1984), p. 67.

3. J. Pieper, *Scholasticism*, transl. Richard and Clara Winston (New York, 1960), p. 63.

4. J. Brady, *A Philosopher's Search for the Infinite* (New York, 1983), pp. 13-71.

5. Matt. 16:26.

6. J. DeFinance, *Theologia Naturalis* (Rome, 1960), p. 5.

7. S. *Augustine*, City of God, xvi, 2.

8. R. Guardini, *Pascal for Our Time*, transl. Brian Thompson (New York, 1966), p. 38.

9. W. James, Varieties of Religious Experience (New York), p. 411

10. *Ibid.*, p. 468.

11. *Ibid.*, p. 401.

12. J. De Finance, *op. cit.*, p. 15.

13. *Ibid.*, p. 15.

14. *Ibid.*, pp. 15, 16.

15. *Ibid.*, p. 78.

16. *Ibid.*, p. 83.

17. *Ibid.*, pp. 93, 95, 103.

18. *Ibid.*, p. 110.

19. *Ibid.*, p. 115.

20. *Ibid.*, pp. 129, 136.

21. S. Brown, *Alone with God* (New York, 1956), p. 135.

22. J. De Finance, *op. cit.*, p. 129.

23. *Ibid.*, p. 145.

24. A. Huxley, *Perennial Philosophy* (Cleveland, 1962), p. 250.

INDEX

C

D

E

F

Faith
  and reason 50
  vs. intellect 118
First Mover 67, 69
Five Ways 11
Form 17

G

God
  as an idea 17
  of philosophy 15
  of religion 15

H

Heraclitus 68
Hume 63

I

Identity
  law of 40
Intellect 23
  agent 108
  vs. faith 118

J

James 117

K

Kant 49, 98
Kemp Smith 15
Knowledge
  direct 93
  introspective 95
  of being 75
  of quantity 79
  philosophical 14
  reflexive 94
  scientific 63, 89
Korinek 79

OF RELATED INTEREST

The Road To Understanding
More Than Dreamt of in Your Philosophy

Joseph M. Bochenski

There is probably not one person who doesn't philosophize. In everyone's life, there are at least some moments when he or she becomes a philosopher. In fact, all of us do philosophize and, it seems, cannot help but philosophize. Humans are destined to philosophize, whether we want to or not.

To help them walk "their first steps," Joseph Bochenski has written this book. It has been called "the golden classic" of treasured avenues leading into philosophical debates, and has initiated many, many novices into the fascinating world of philosophy. It has come forth from a very popular series of radio lectures – on basic philosophical issues like truth, knowledge, thinking, laws, values, humanity, society, and God – taking us from Plato to Wittgenstein, from Kant to Aristotle, and back. And you don't feel overwhelmed at all!

"Few have the philosophical breadth or clarity of expression characteristic of Bochenski's work. In this extraordinary introduction to philosophy, Bochenski with admirable precision and brevity presents a spectrum of philosophical issues, rendering them accessible to the beginner. His judgments flow from the great Aristotelian-Thomistic tradition, updated by the author himself."
  Jude P. Dougherty, Dean of the School of Philosophy, The Catholic University of America.

Joseph M. Bochenski, O.P., is one of the most prominent logicians of this century. He received his doctorate in philosophy from the University of Fribourg (Switzerland). He taught logic at the Angelicum in Rome and philosophy at the University of Fribourg (Switzerland). He was also a visiting professor at the University of Notre Dame, the University of California at L.A., the University of Kansas, and the University of Pittsburgh.

5.25" x 8.5"; 128 pages with index
ISBN 1-886670-06-4 softbound $ 13.95

OF RELATED INTEREST

by
William Van der Zee

APE OR ADAM?
Our Roots
According to
the Book of Genesis

DELIVER US FROM EVIL
Is Something Wrong
Between God and Me?

These are the ideal books for personal meditation and reflection, for discussion groups and Bible studies; for people who love God, as well as for those who struggle with Him; for those who are searching and questioning, as well as for those who have found God, or think they have. The author, Rev. William Van der Zee, has become well known and highly respected for his famous radio and television talks on hot topics in the Bible. His books, which have had many reprints in Europe, have the right blend of pastorship and scholarship; they are uplifting, and yet down to earth.

Ape or Adam?
Our Roots According to the Book of Genesis

The first book of the bible is not about the world's origin – as to how it happened and when it happened – which is food for scientists. The bible is not an old book on modern science; it has actually two different stories on the creation of human beings. If one took them as a literal or scientific account of some actual events in the past, the two stories would directly contradict one another. Apparently, these stories do not in any way claim to be an eye-witness account. They are stories – not fables – that try to clarify the unique relationship between human beings and their Creator.

The book of Genesis is not about the *origin* of everything but about the *creation* of everything. Therefore, it is impossible for the book of Genesis to come in conflict with any scientific theory whatsoever – just as in turn no scientific discovery is ever capable of dethroning God or refuting the biblical testimony. In reading this book, you come to the sudden awareness that bible and science, faith and knowledge do not contradict each other. It doesn't matter any longer whether we decide on creation or evolution: It is God who is at the beginning and will be at the end. Our choice is not between *Adam* and *ape*, but between the *old Adam* and the *new Adam*. Adam is you and me. And with this in mind, we open that old book again...

120 pages with index   ISBN 1-886670-03-X softbound $ 19.50

Deliver Us from Evil
Is Something Wrong between God and Me?

To humanists, Marxists, and Buddhists, suffering may be equally painful as it is to Jews and Christians, but the former are not haunted with this piercing question, this agonizing riddle, "For what reason?" Believing in a God of love, in a good creation, and in His providence, causes the pain of suffering to penetrate to a much deeper level: Why does it strike *me*? Is something wrong between God and me?

If there is one book in particular that has struggled with this question, it's the book about an honest, just, and rebellious man called Job, being entirely ruined. His friends say it was God who ruined him; in order to punish him, some say; in order to teach him, others say.

From age to age, people have been comforted by thoughts such as these. No matter how bad things get, at least there is a purpose to it all. Job, however, did not find comfort in these thoughts. From beginning to end, he keeps searching for God. He actually reverses the question – from: How just am *I*? to: How just is *God*? Never before Job was there such a fierce ring to the question as to what God has to do with our afflictions – when bad things happen to good people.

The author of this book takes us through all of Job's agonies, as though they were ours. To the very end, to God's answer.

128 pages with index   ISBN 1-886670-02-1 softbound $ 14.95

The Physicists and God
The New Priests of Religion?
by
Anthony Van den Beukel

The universe is a collection of microscopically small particles which developed at the very beginning from a Big Bang. Scientists can describe very precisely how all this came about. It makes breathtaking reading, but one's heart remains cold. What are human beings really? And where is God in all this? "As a physicist you have to have a split personality still to be able to believe in a God," said a recent winner of a Noble Prize for science.

Being a professor of physics and a researcher for 30 years, at a prestigious university, the author of *The Physicists and God* is one of those physicists with a supposedly split personality himself. In this book, he investigates what kind of reality physicists are occupied with. Science seems to strive for a comprehensive explanation of the world in which we live. If that is the case, then belief in God will be ruled out. But is it really the *whole* of reality? If scientists ever finish their work, will they then understand *everything*? Or are there, as Hamlet says to Horatio, "more things in heaven and earth than are dreamt of in your philosophy?"

Taking issue with recent scientific writers on this theme, the author of this book looks not only at recent developments in science but also at scientists themselves, and the motivations behind their scientific activities. The result is a fascinating survey of modern science and an encouraging indication that the possibility of meaningful religious belief is still very much there.

"Professor Van den Beukel seems to me to be a very honest man, thinking seriously about science as a human enterprise, which is the way I like to think about it, and not as some disembodied collection of abstractions which have no connection with ordinary life. This is a book well worth reading."
C.W. Francis Everitt, Professor of Experimental Physics, Stanford University.

"In his book Anthony Van den Beukel faces the question whether physics and religion are compatible. His answer is as sincere as it is convincing [...] The book is worth reading just for the mere fact that it explains the new physics in simple language [...] It is a marvelous book that I read in one and the same breath."
Frans Saris, Professor of Physics at the University of Utrecht and Director of the Amsterdam Institute for Fundamental Research on Matter.

"Something funny is happening to physics. As more and more is discovered about the early universe and the structure of matter, so the debate about the role of God in it all intensifies [...] This book is a surprisingly emotional testimony [...] It is a powerful argument."
Angela Tilby, Producer for BBC television

"[...] an interesting contribution to the literature on science and religion."
John Polkinghorne, President of Queens' College and former Professor of Mathematical Physics at Cambridge University.

200 pages with index   ISBN 1-886670-01-3 softbound $ 24.50

Life Scientists
Their Convictions, Their Activities, and Their Values.
by
Gerard M. Verschuuren

Life scientists appear to be the wizards of this new era. They have ventured to tackle issues ranging from the origin of life to the origins of humankind; from medical and genetic knowledge to questions about how to control life and death. Spectacular are the achievements they have made. Who are these scientists? How do they operate? What do they believe? What do they value?

Science is no more objective and rational than the humans who do it. This book shows us the "world" of life scientists, seen through the eyes of a biologist with a philosophical background. It's a guided tour through the philosophy of the life sciences, based on the insights of modern scholarship, without going into unnecessary technicalities. The author was characterized by Michael Ruse, in *Nature*, as someone having "a happy knack of laying out positions quickly and clearly; [... and having] a real gift for setting down an idea diagrammatically, separating out concepts with a few strokes of the pen."

"This book [...] demonstrates the author's extensive and profound knowledge of biology. I enjoy the (brief) historical context in which he places the issues at hand and the clear-headed philosophical analysis. The writing is succinct, clear, eminently didactic."

Francisco J. Ayala, Dept. of Ecology and Evolutionary Biology, University of California, Irvine (Cal.)

"As important as biology is today, most books in the philosophy of biology are too technical to be understood by students and the general public. In *Life Scientists*, Verschuuren gives his readers the benefits of his deep understanding of recent work in both biology and philosophy without burdening his exposition with unnecessary technicalities. Anyone who is interested in current thinking in the philosophy of biology will profit from reading this book."

David L. Hull, Dept. of Philosophy, Northwestern University, Evanston (Ill.)

288 pages with index   ISBN 1-886670-00-5 hardcover $ 34.50